# ❧ OWL ❧
## COLORING BOOK
## FOR ADULTS

▲ **ART** THERAPY COLORING

# Preview of Coloring Pages

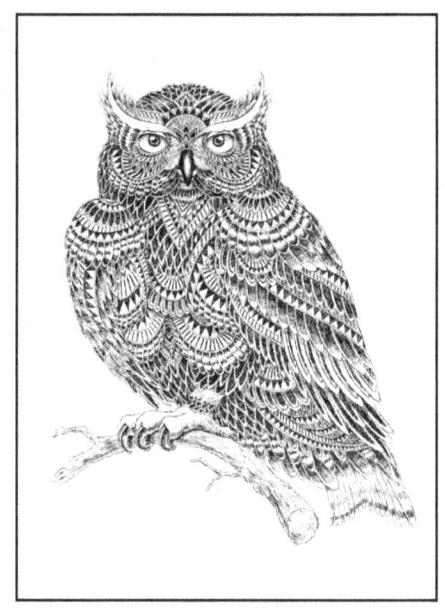
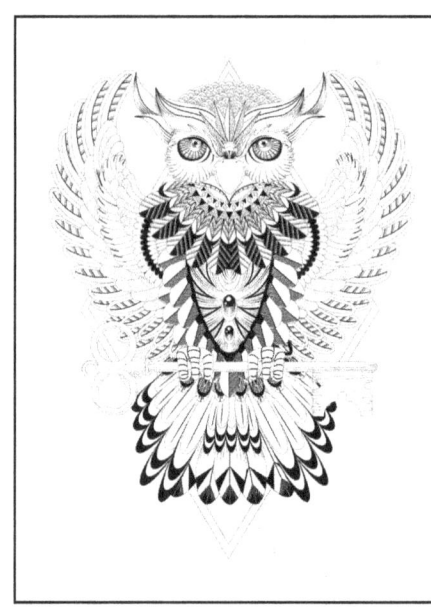
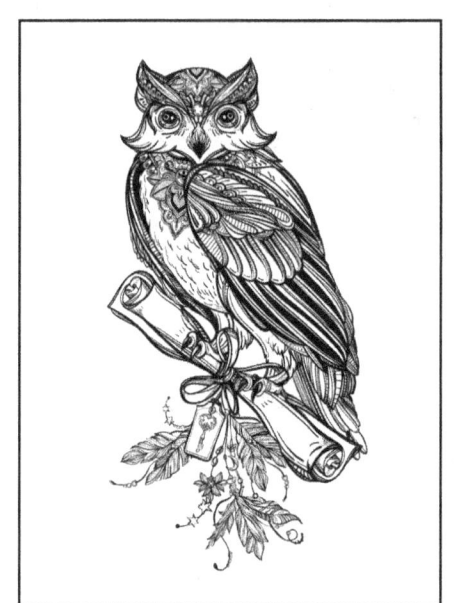
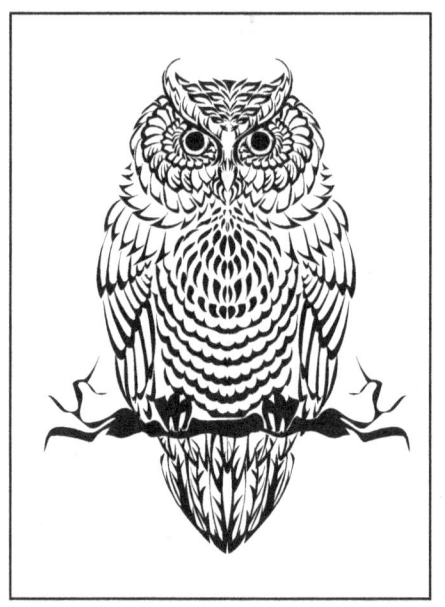
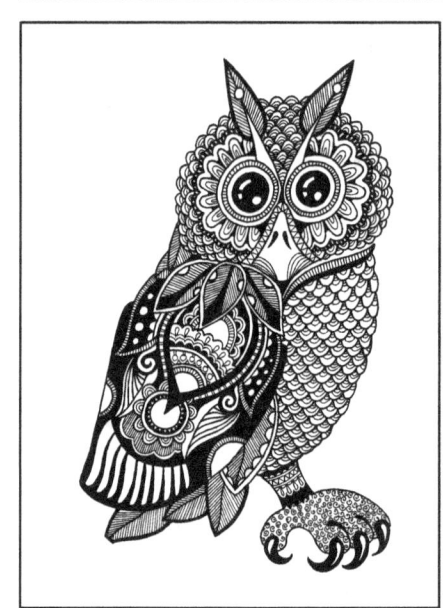
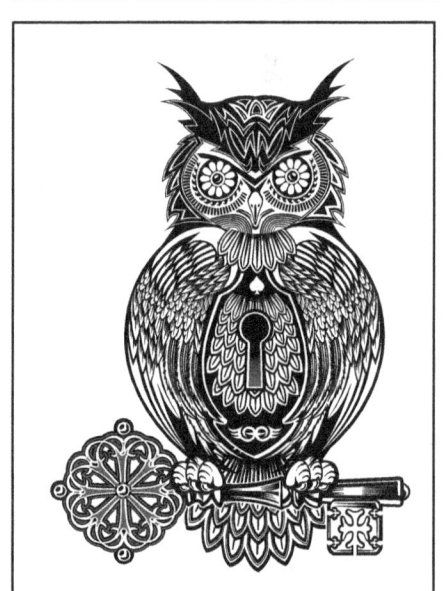
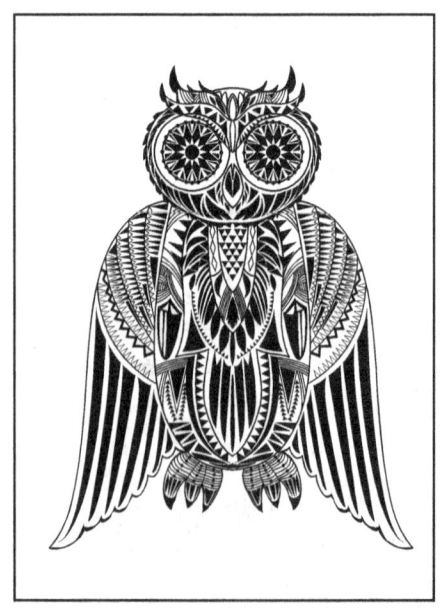
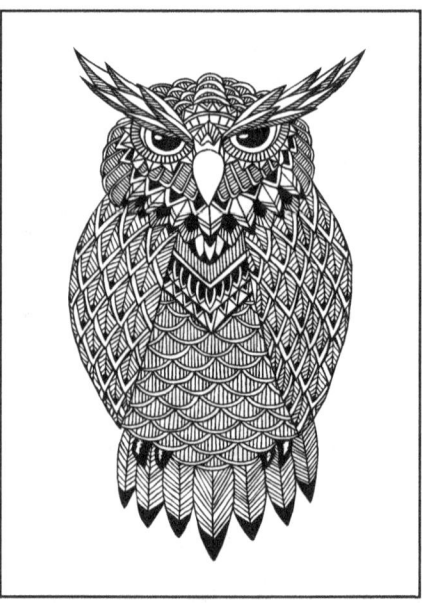
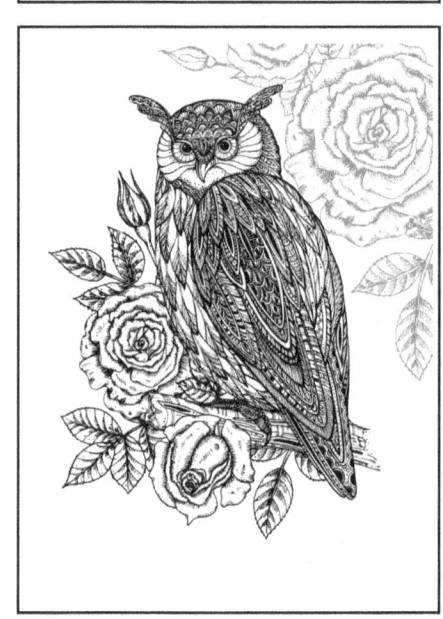

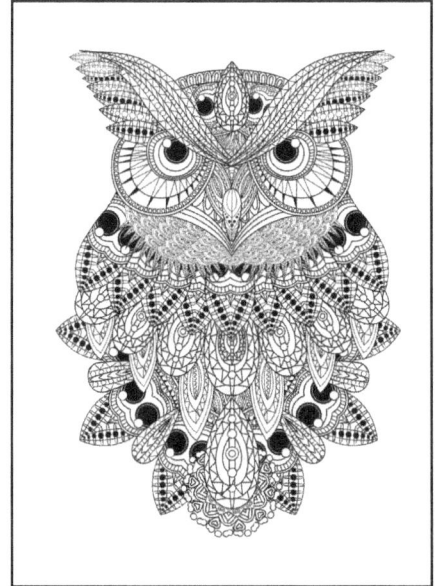
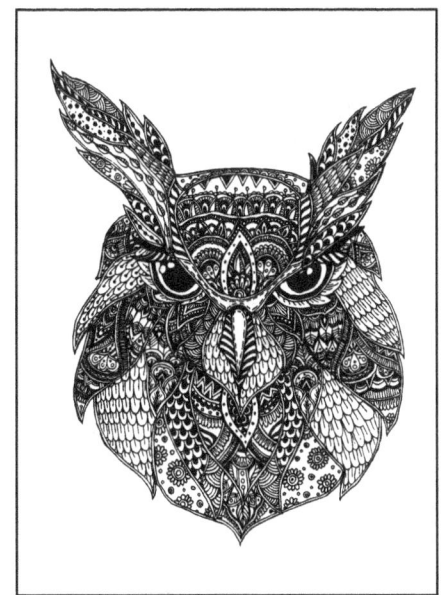
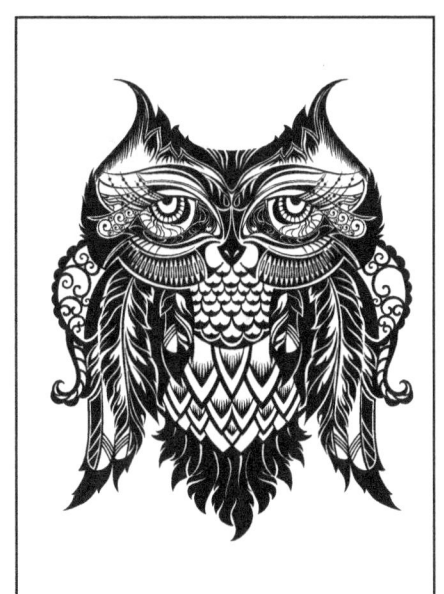
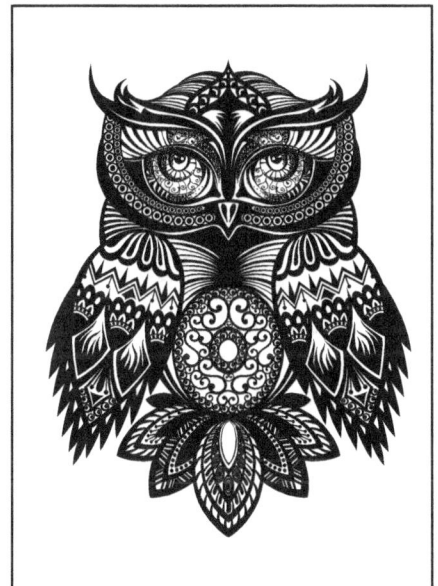
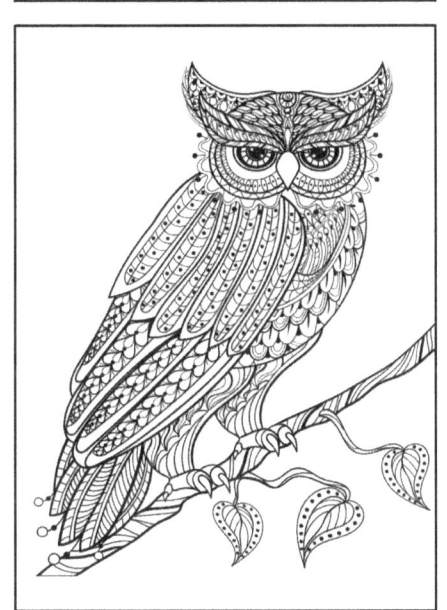
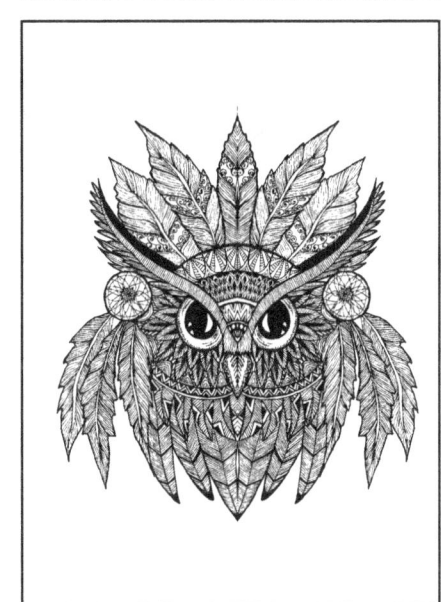
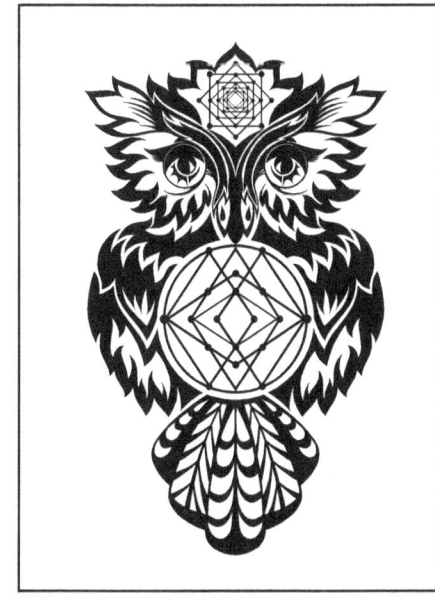
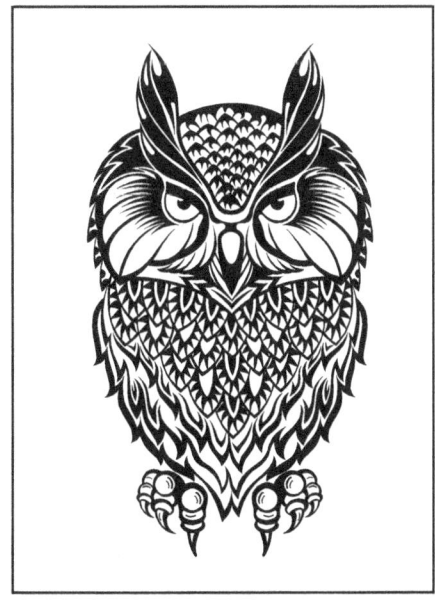
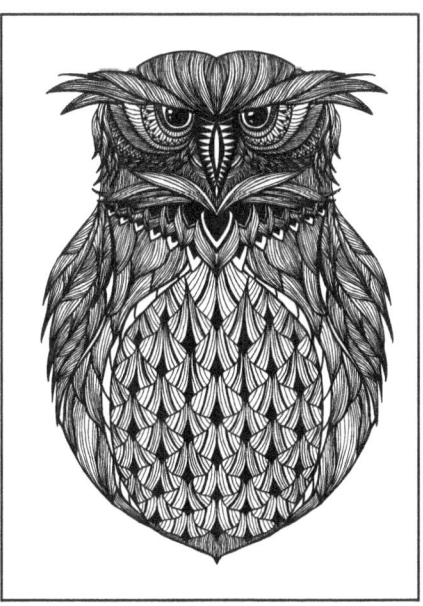

# Preview of Coloring Pages

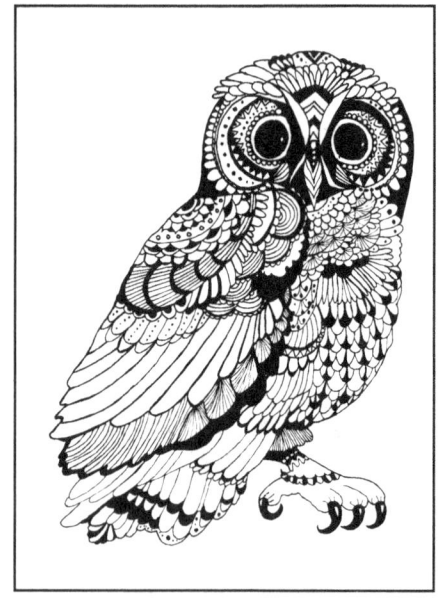
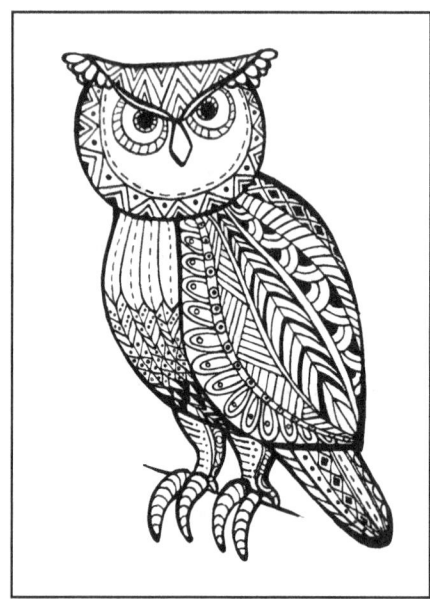
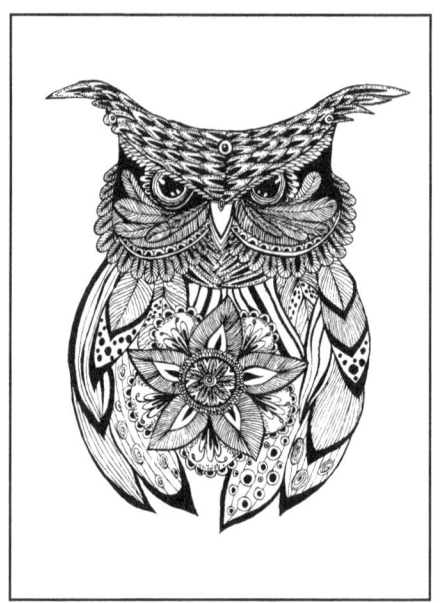
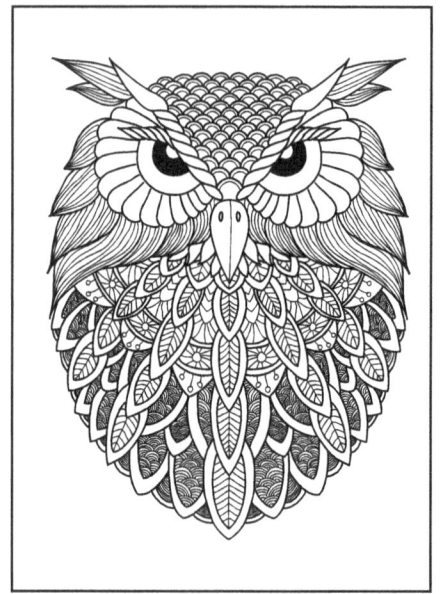
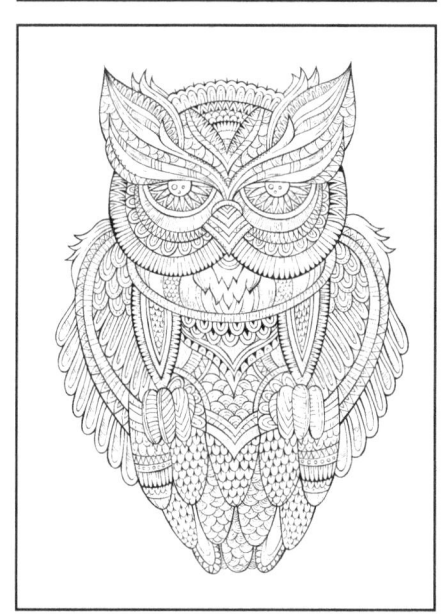
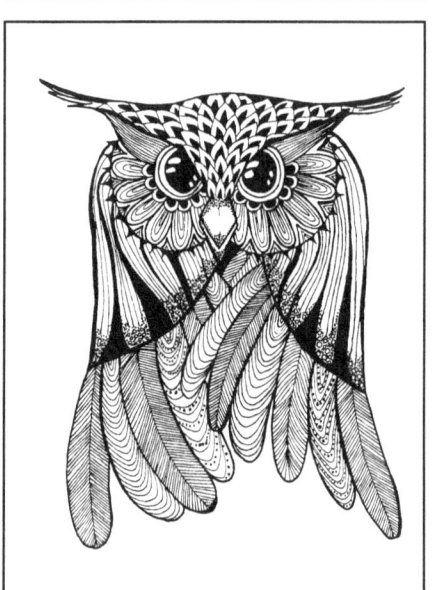
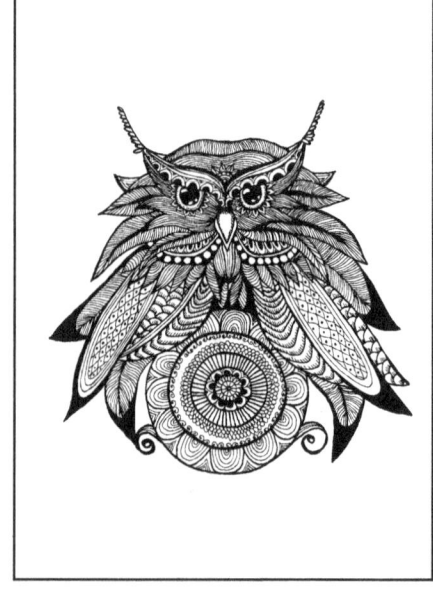
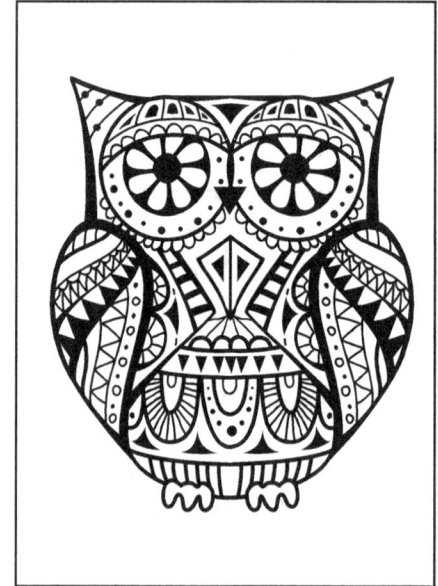
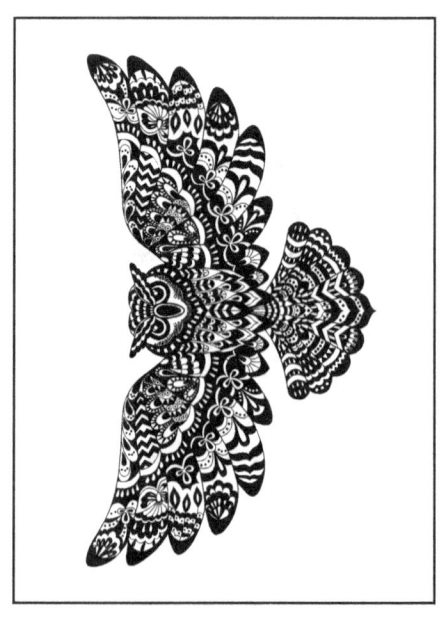

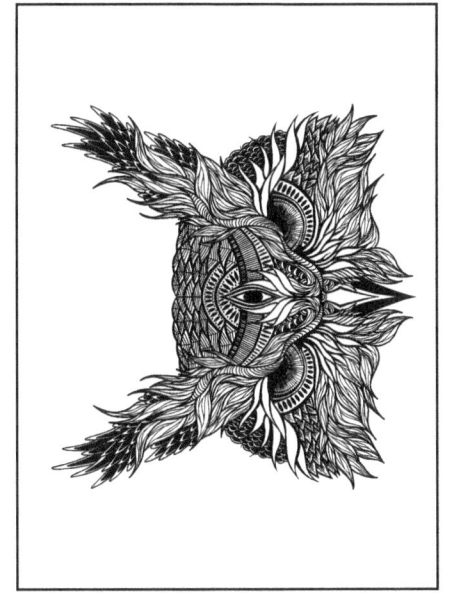
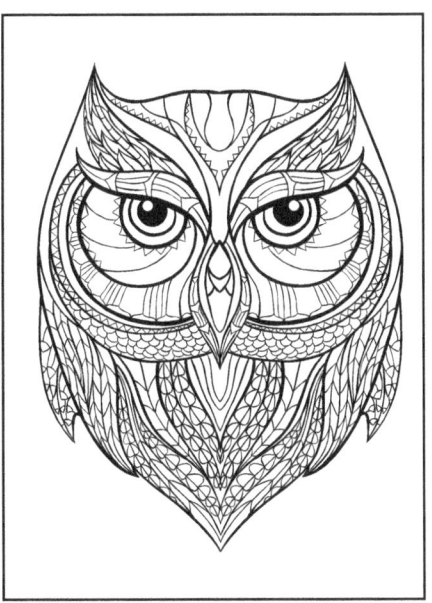
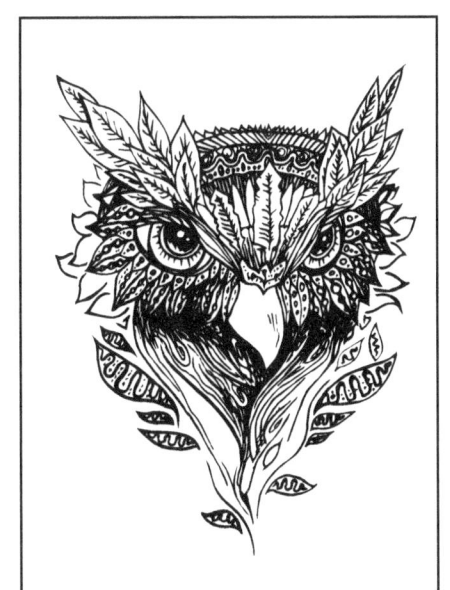
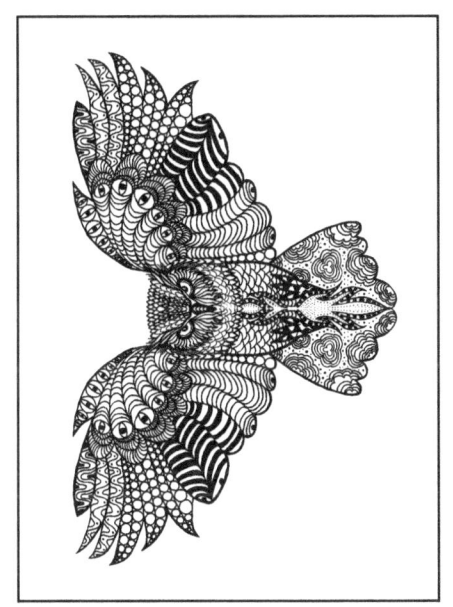
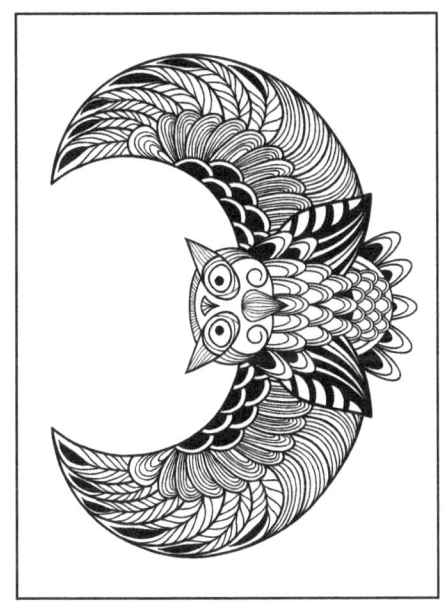
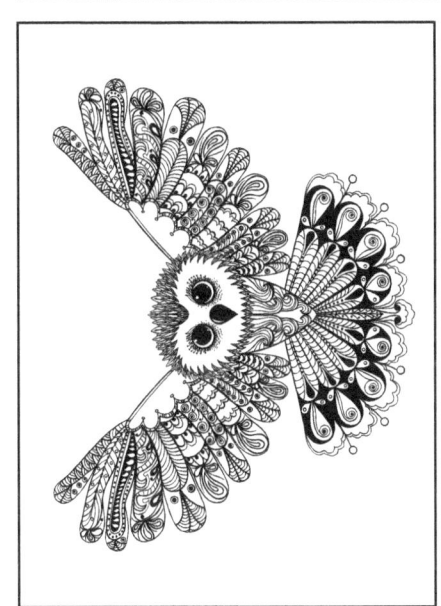
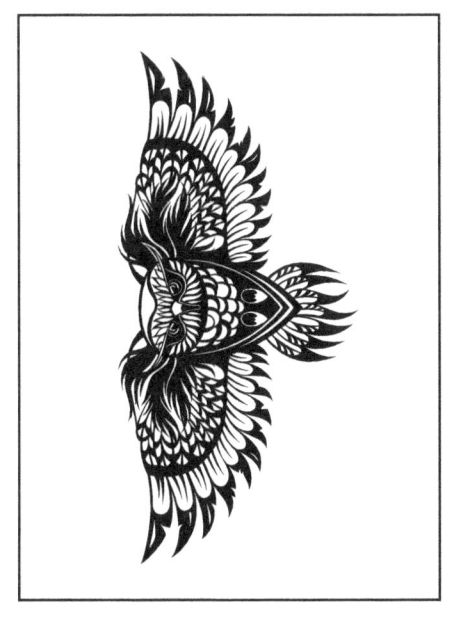
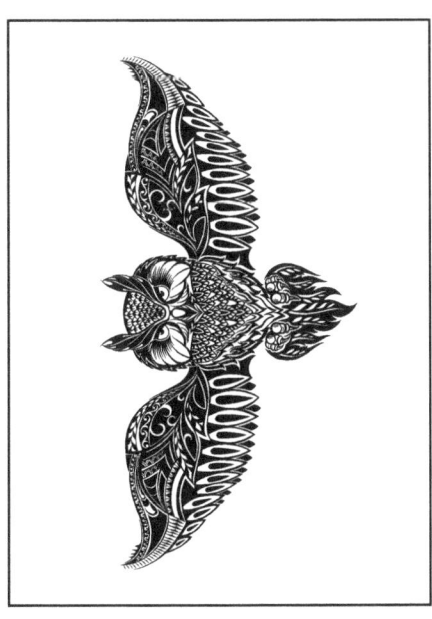
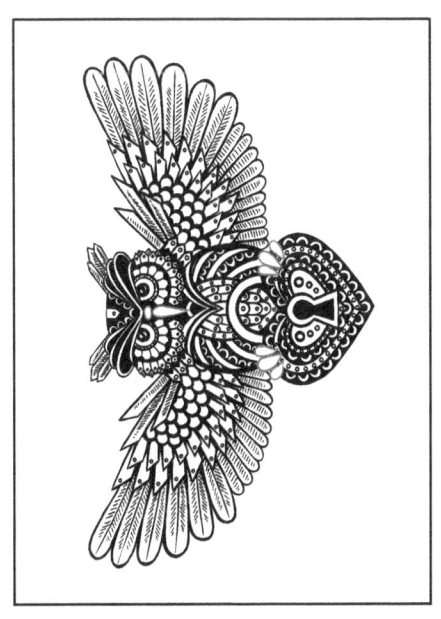

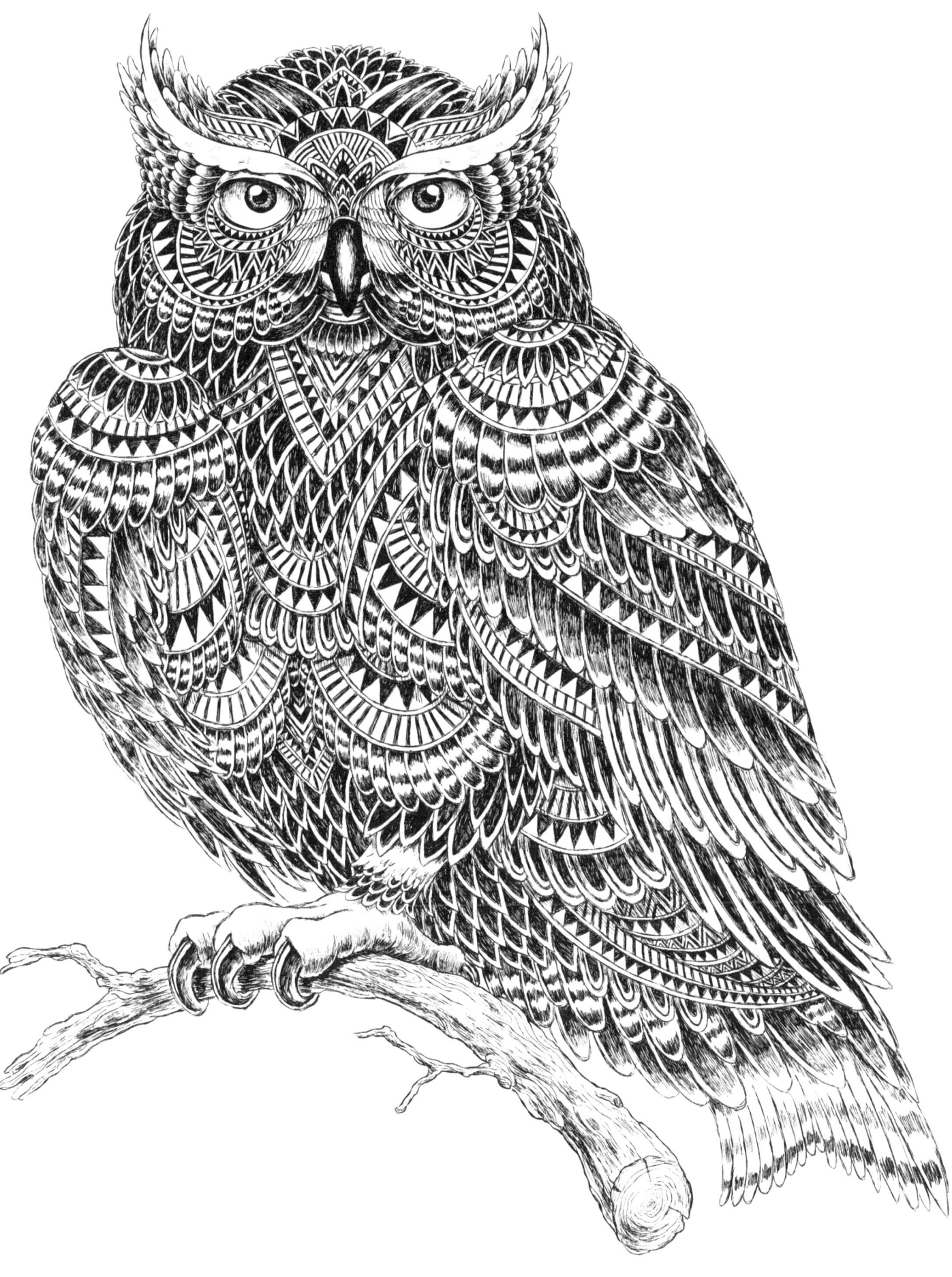

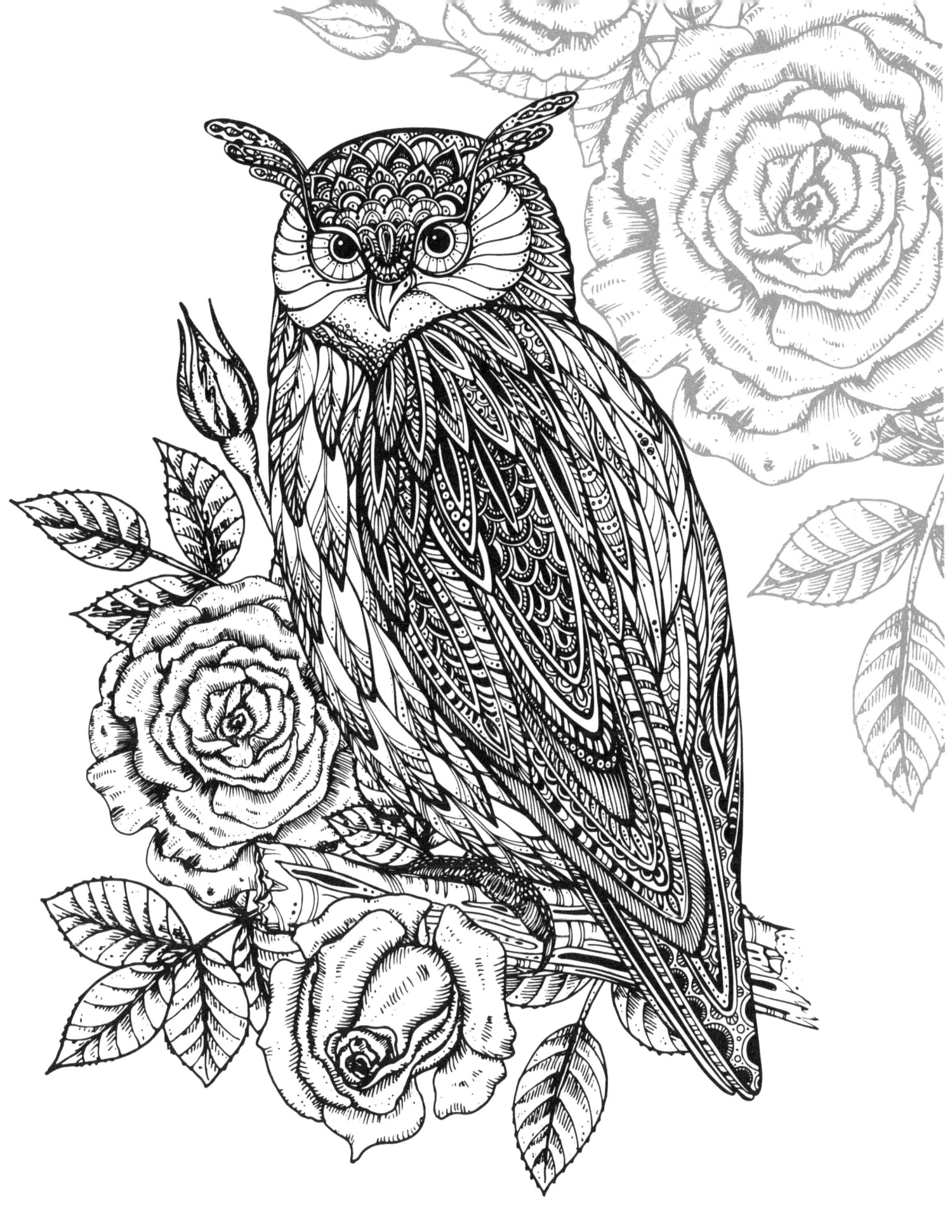

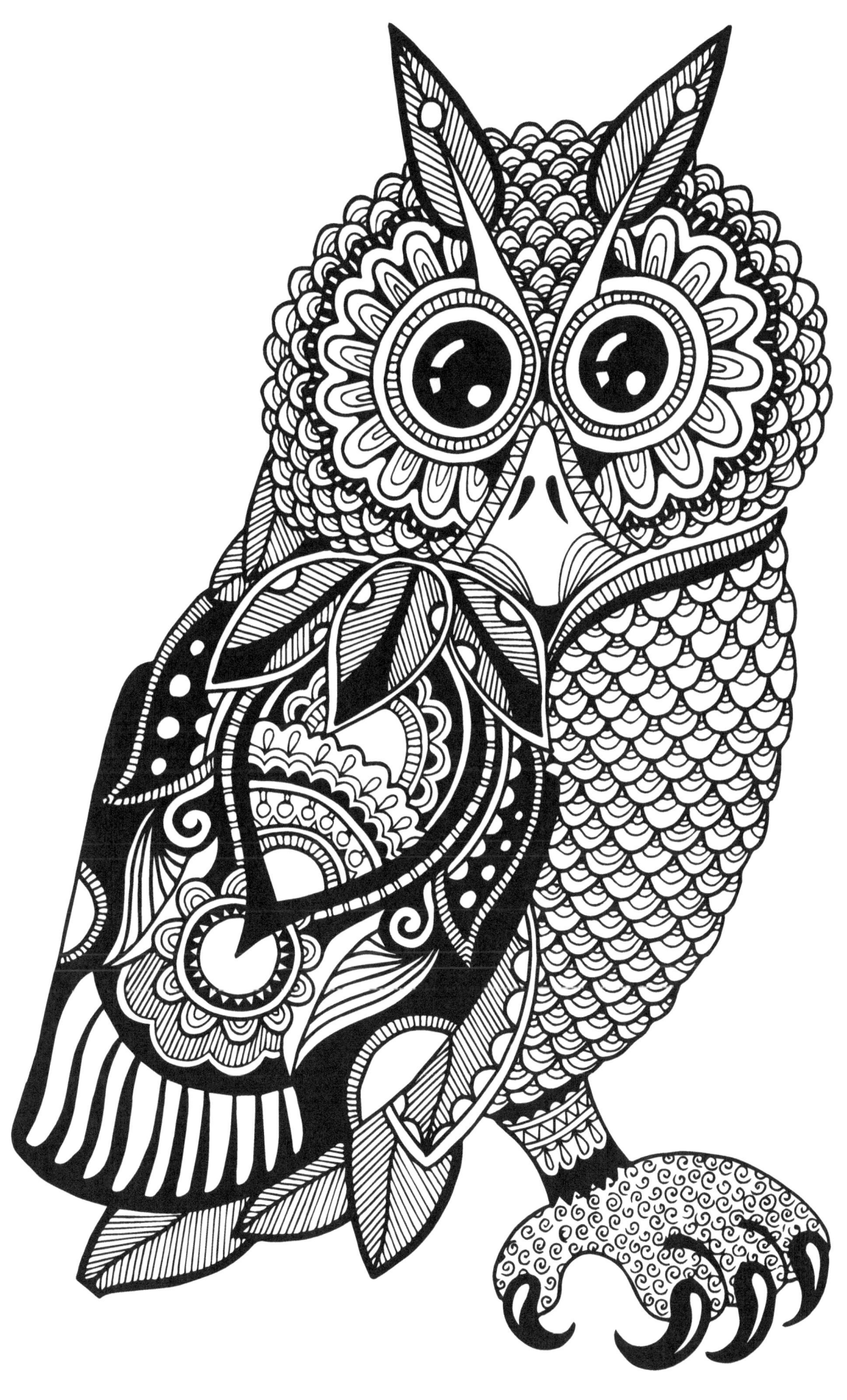

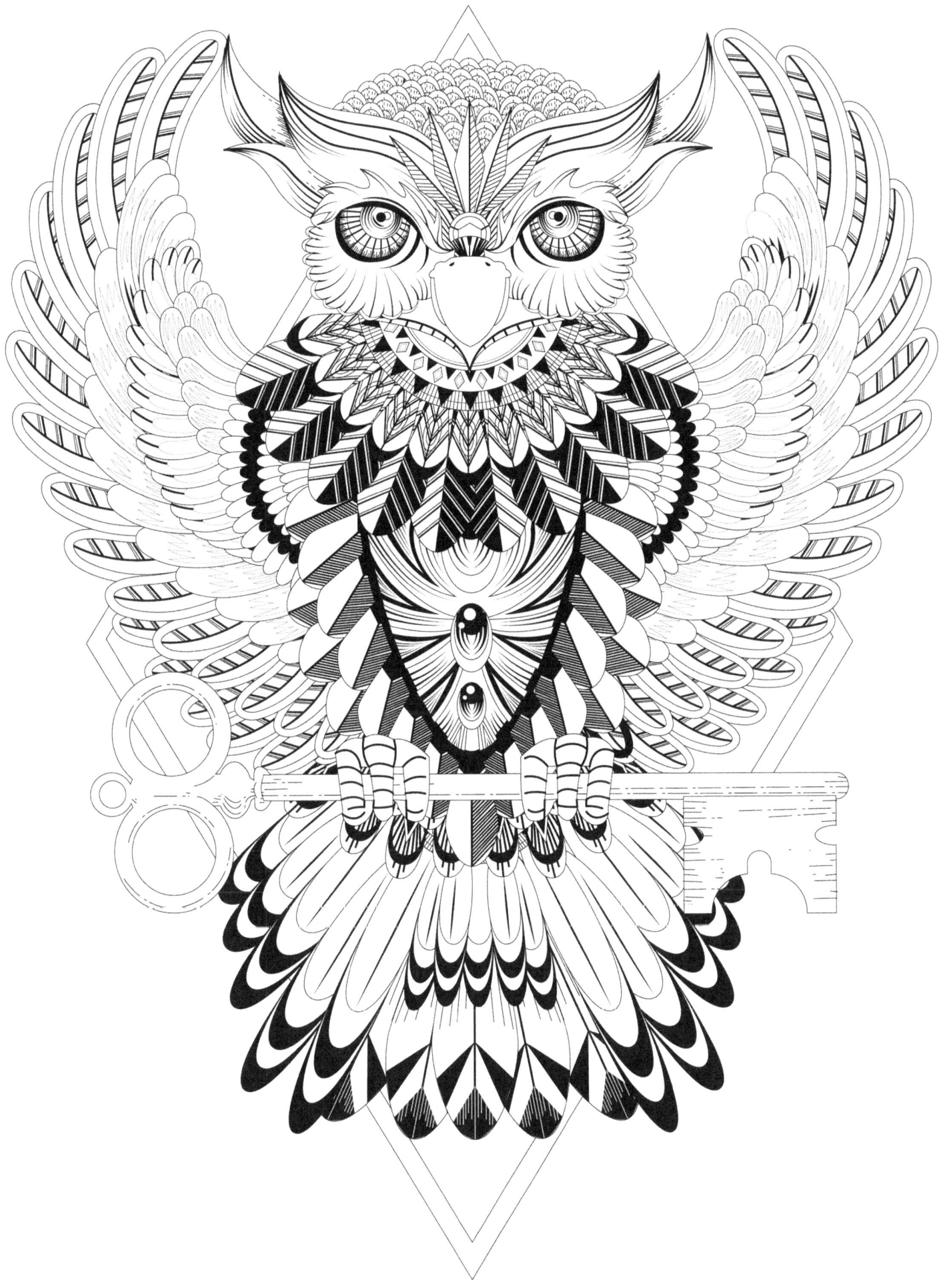

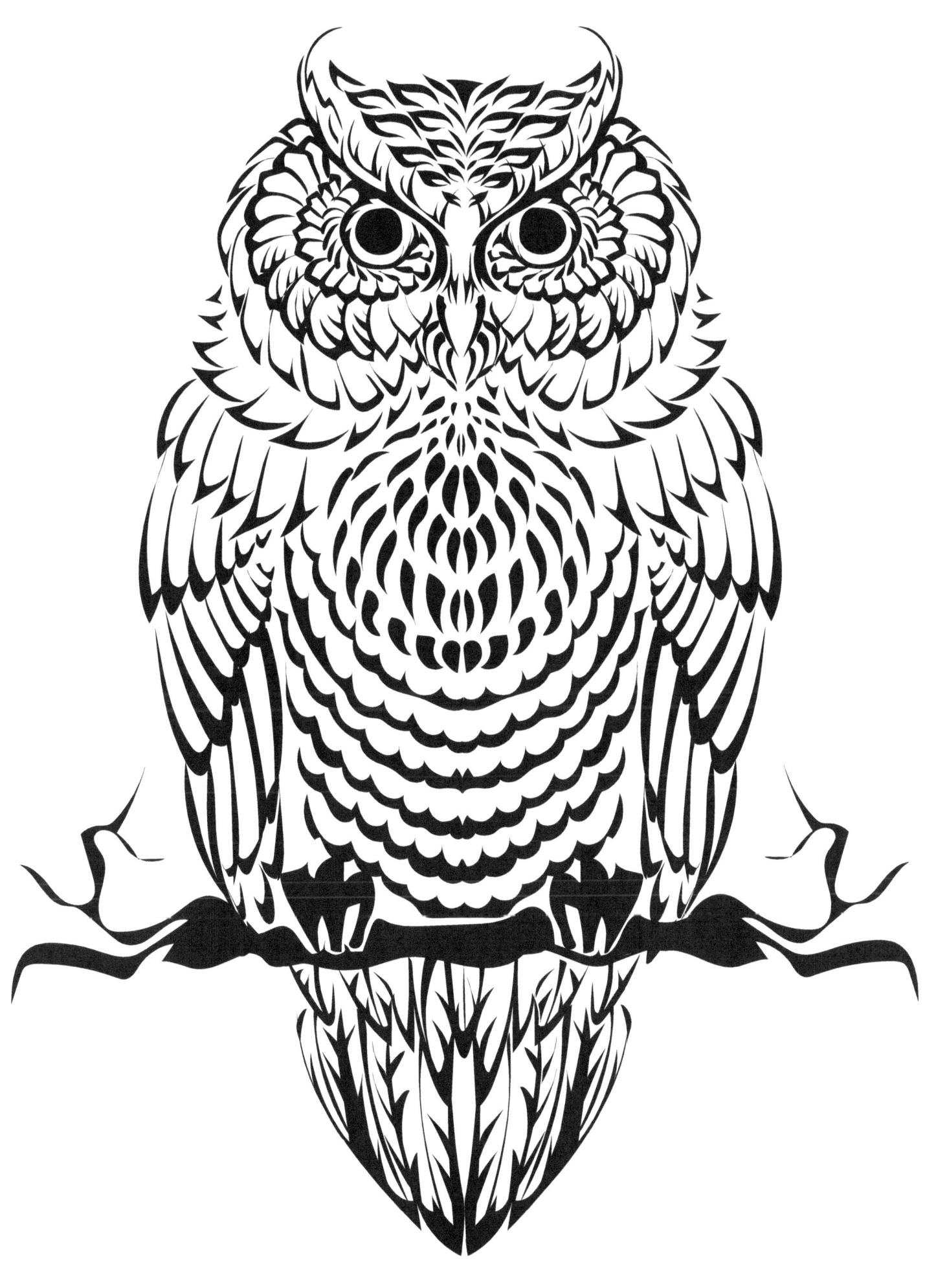

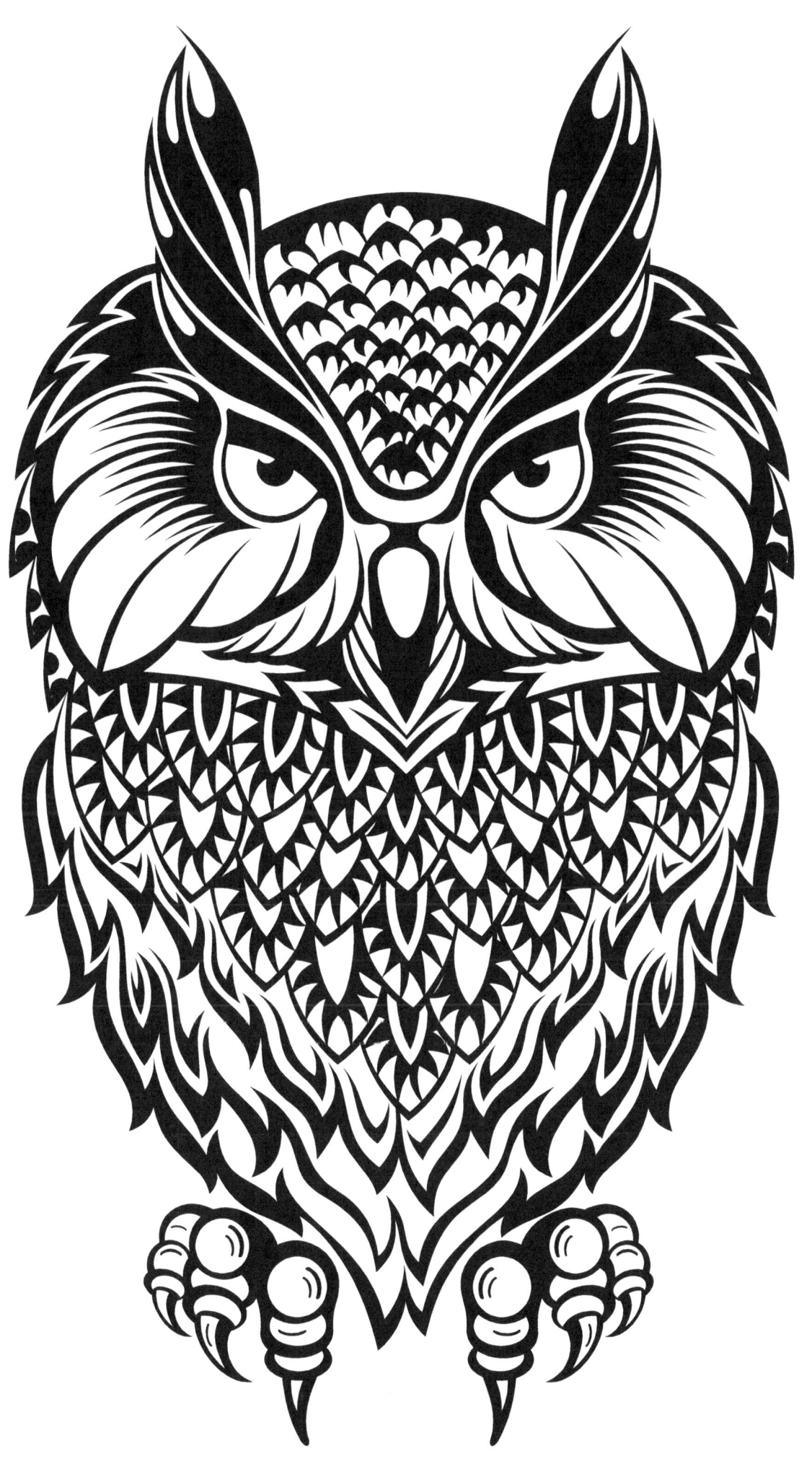

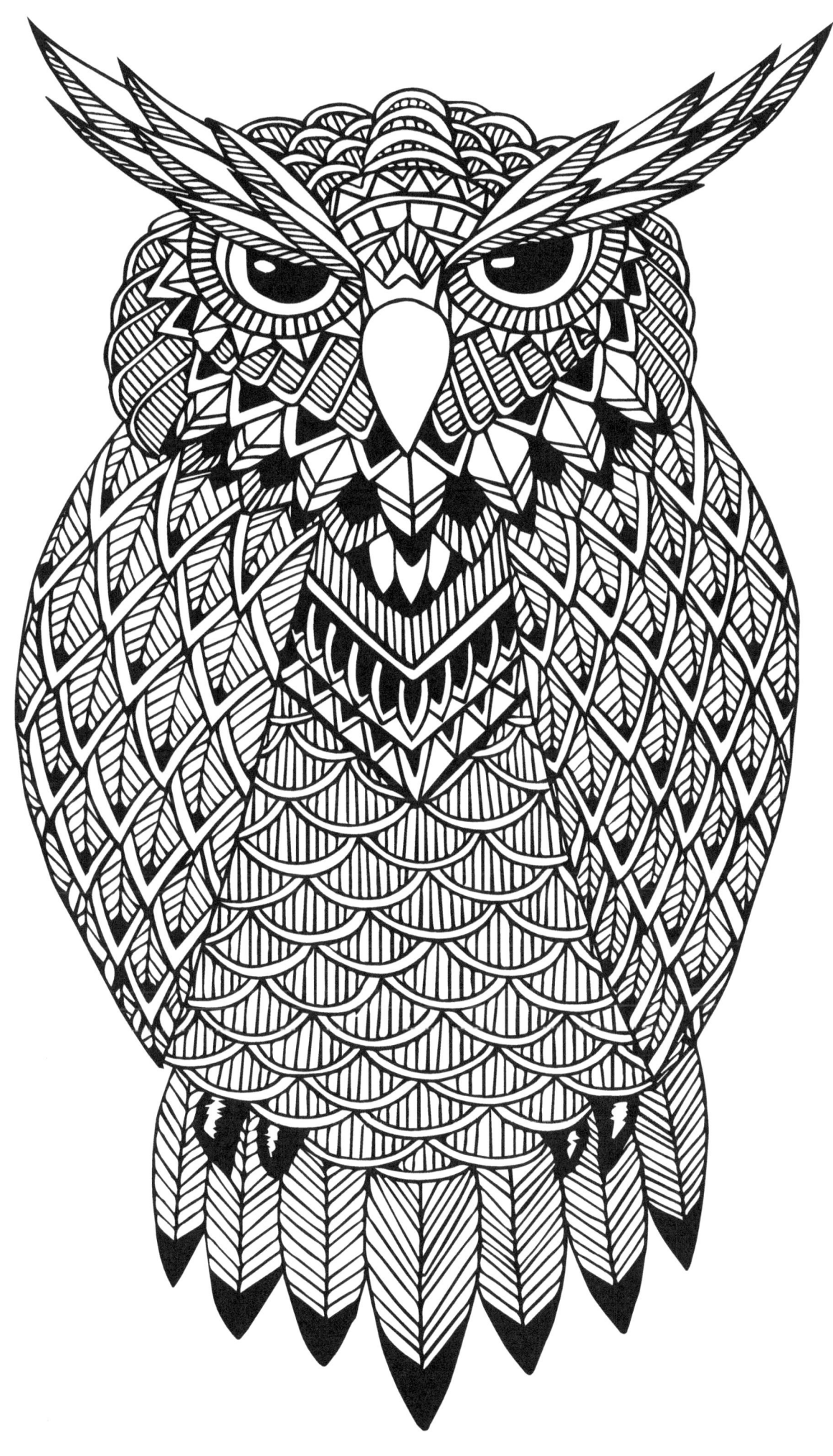

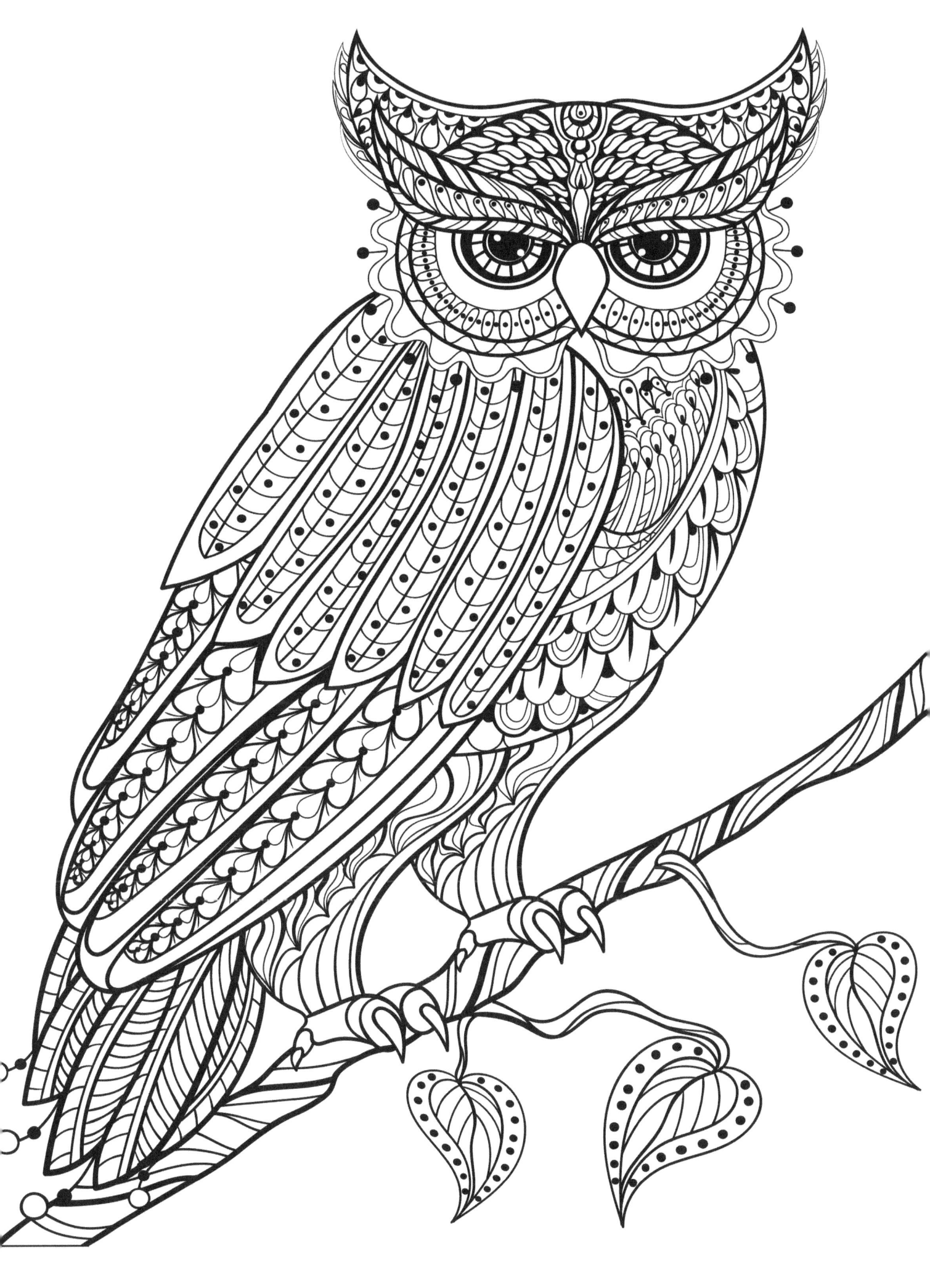

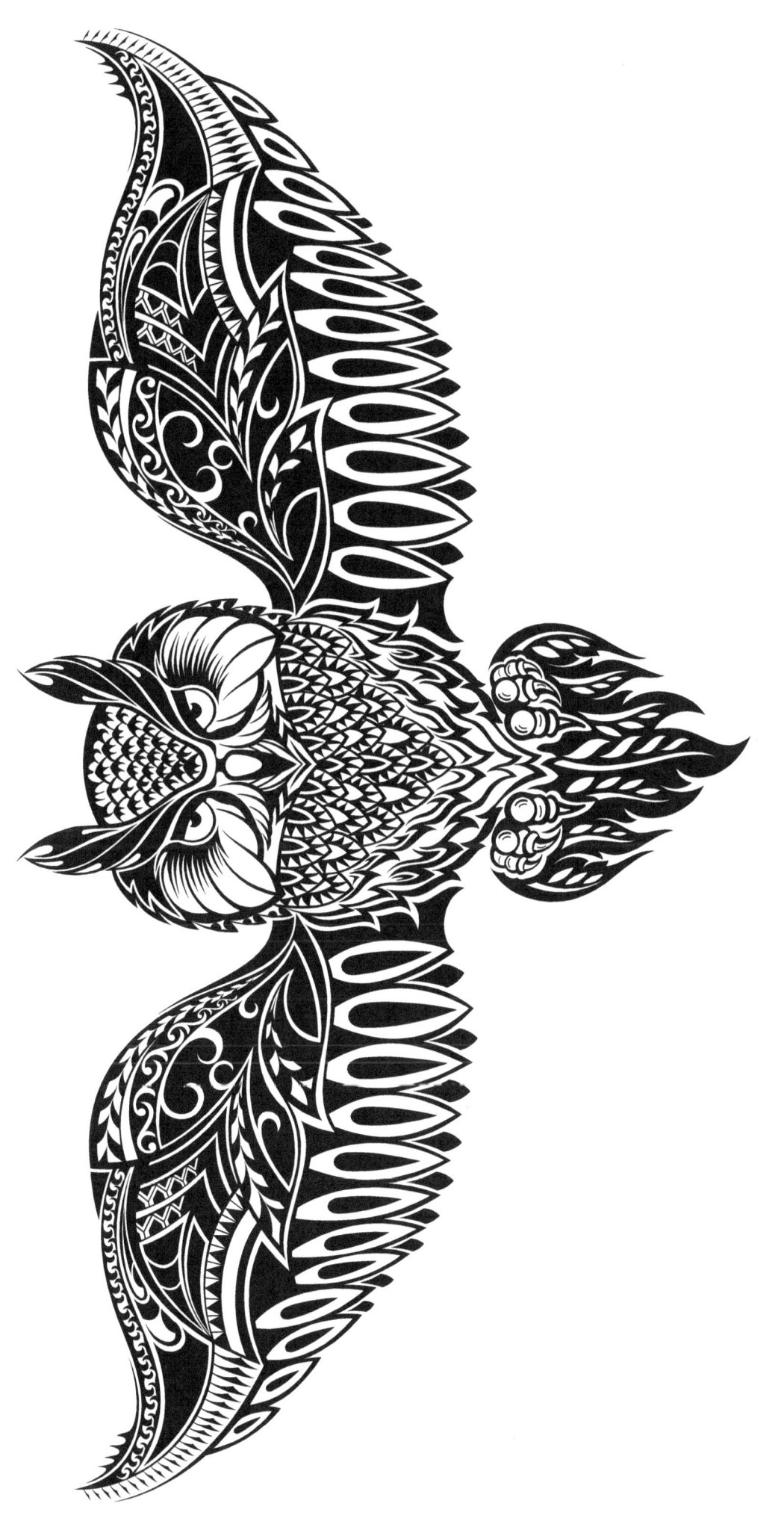

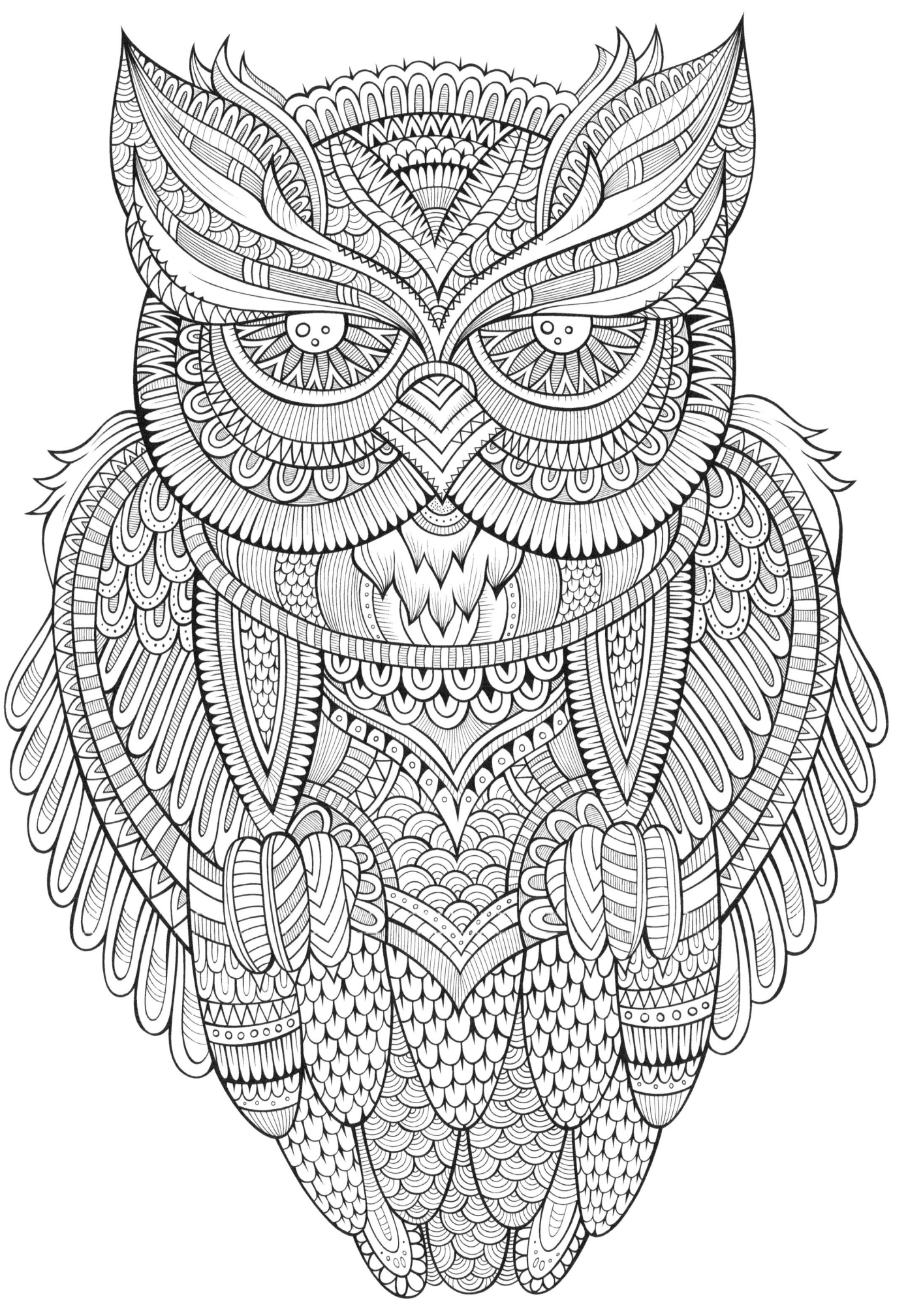

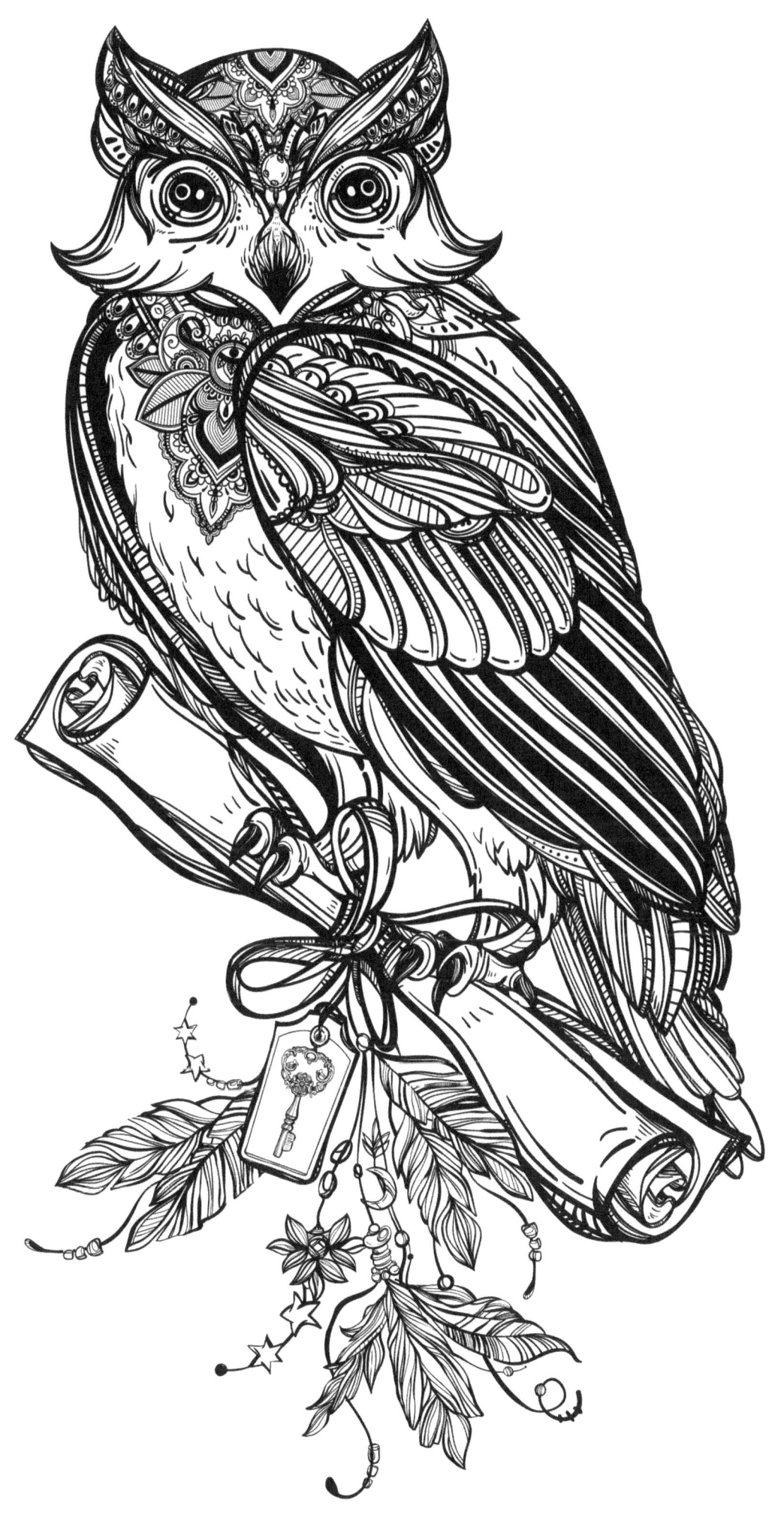

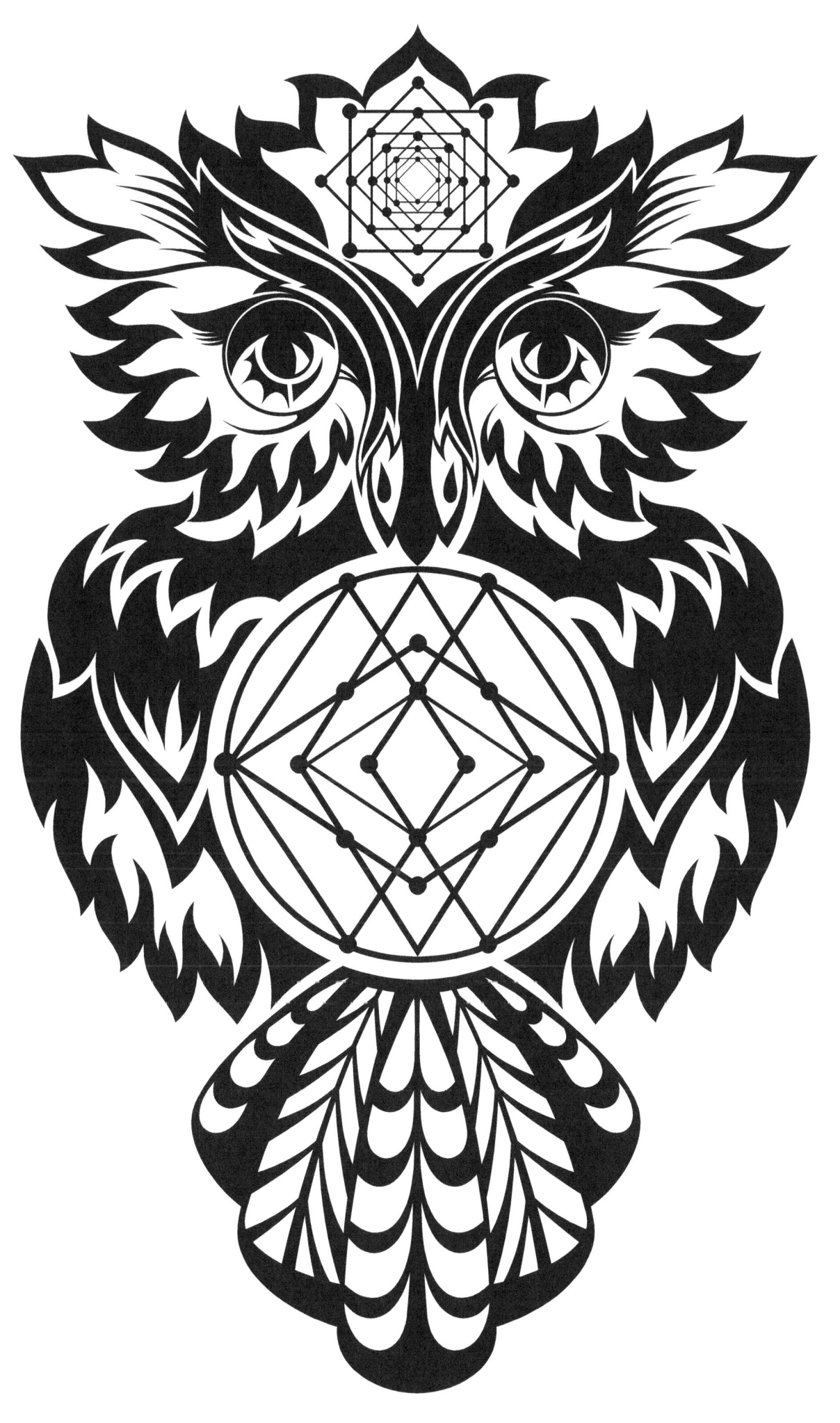

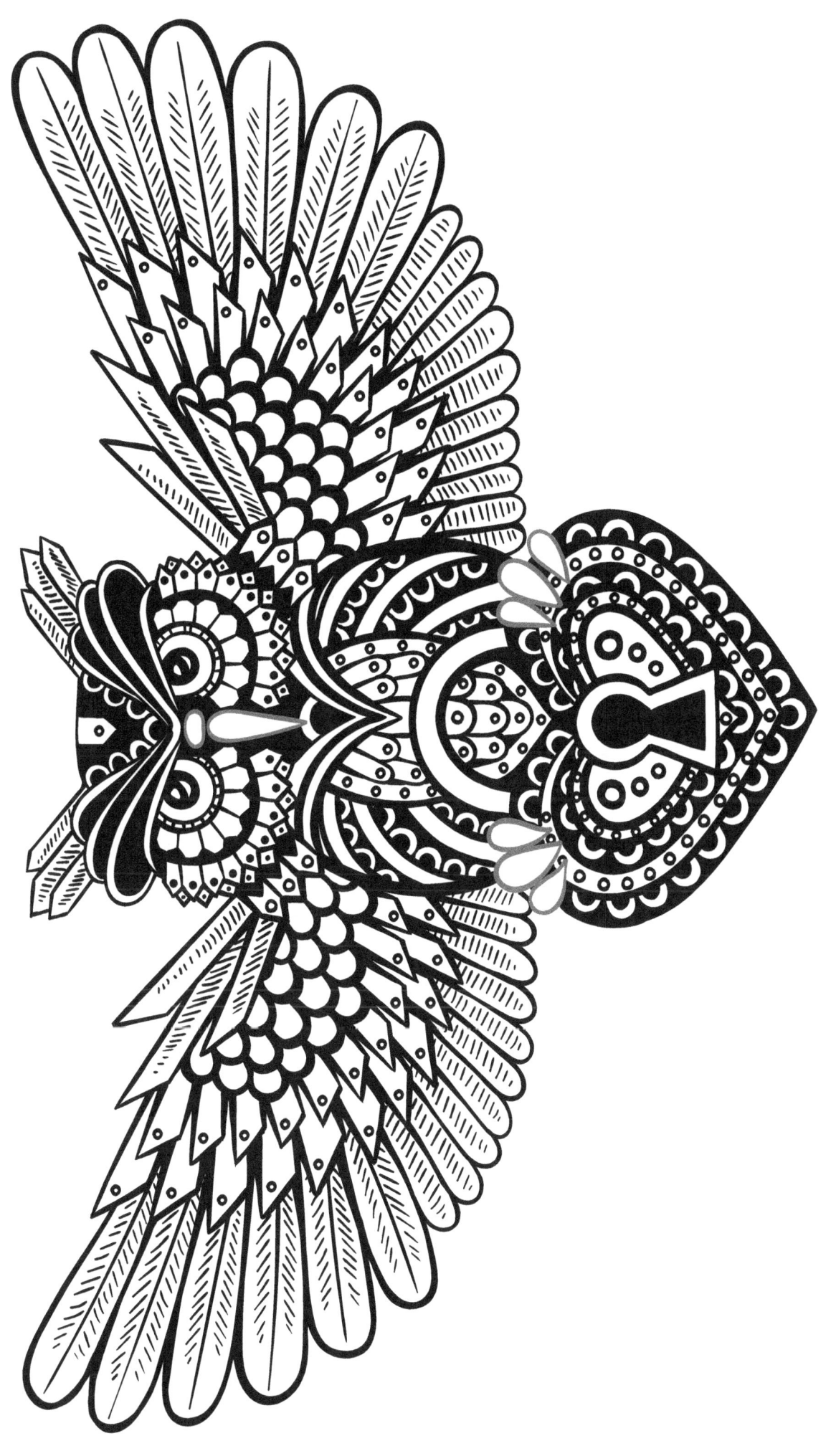

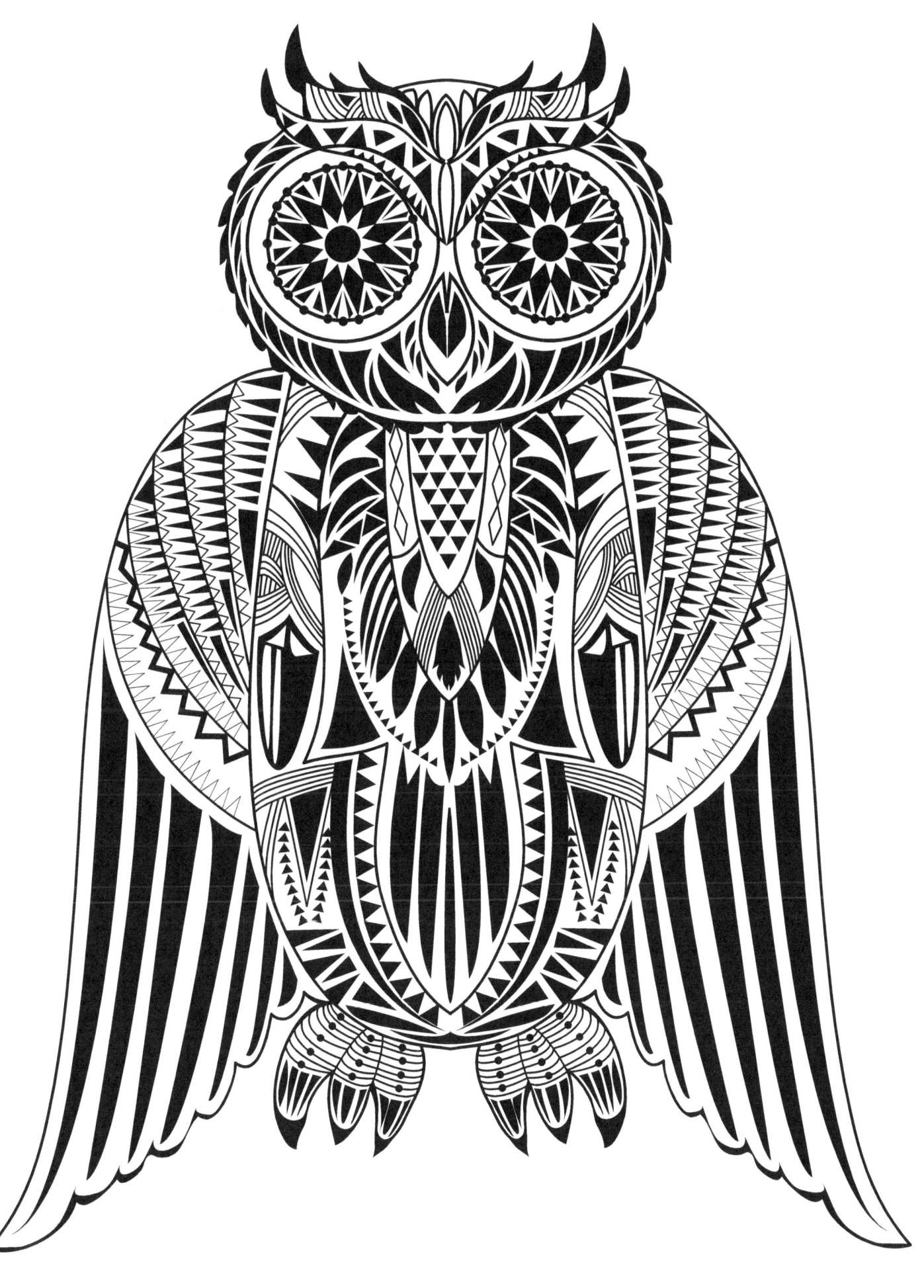

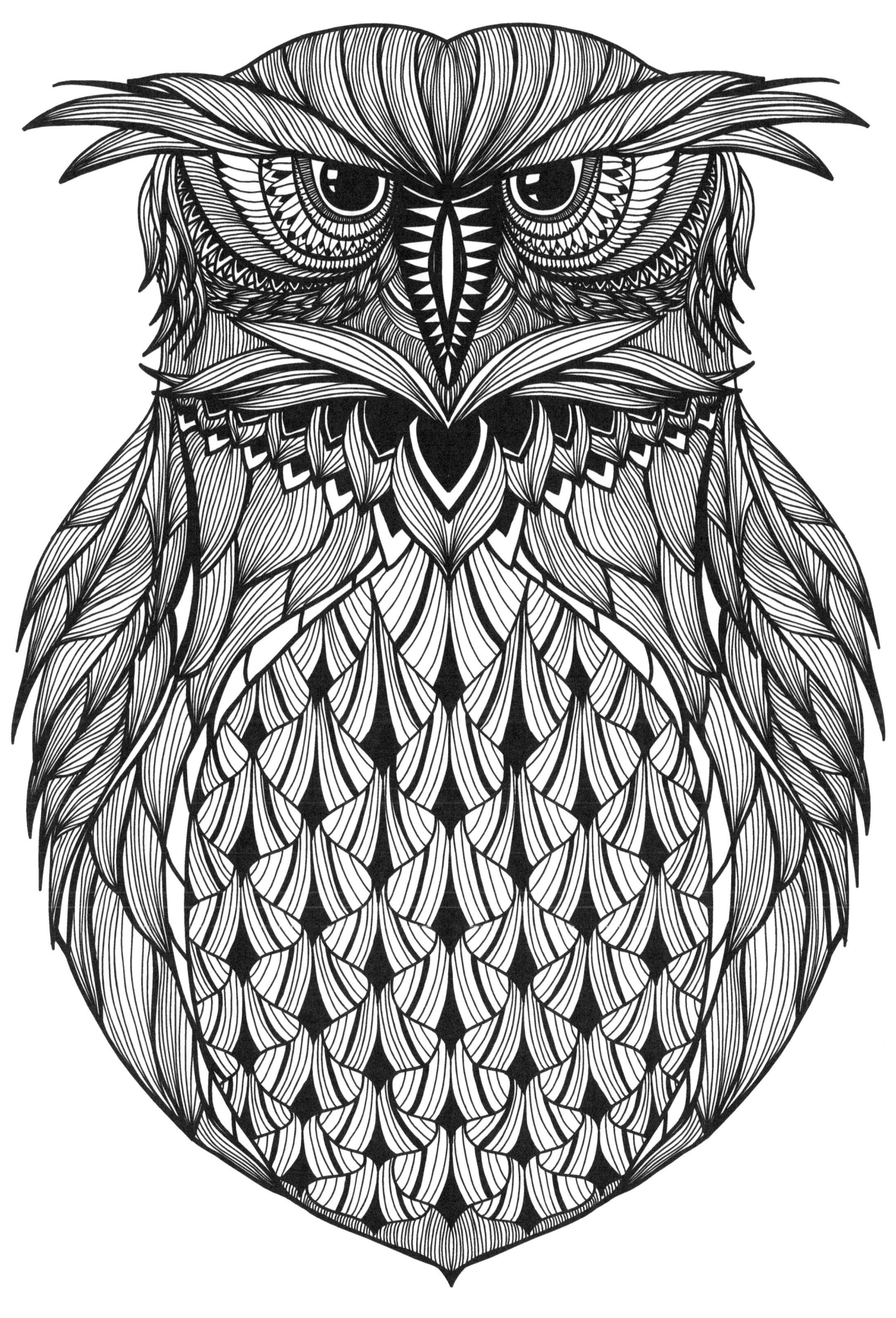

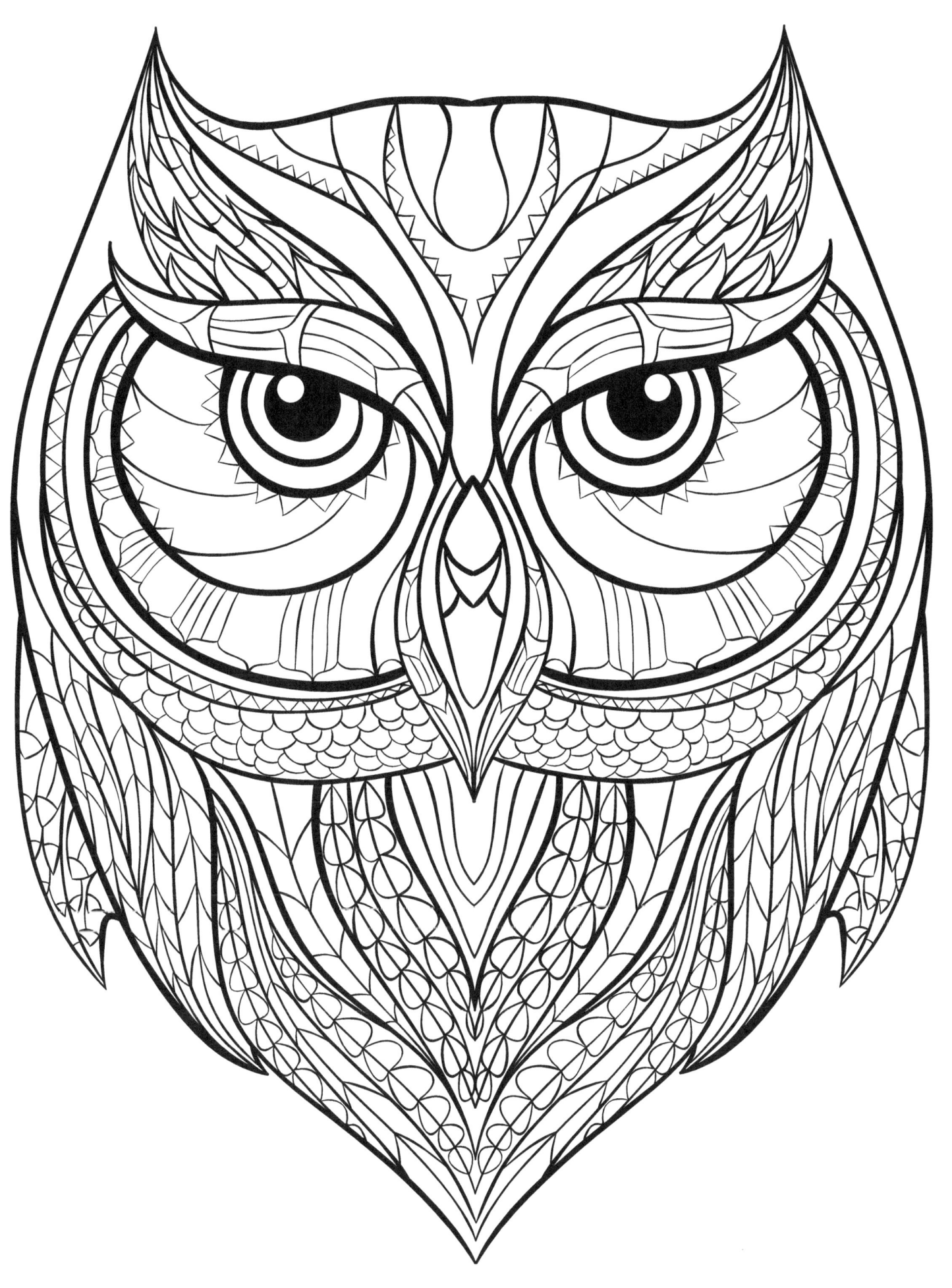

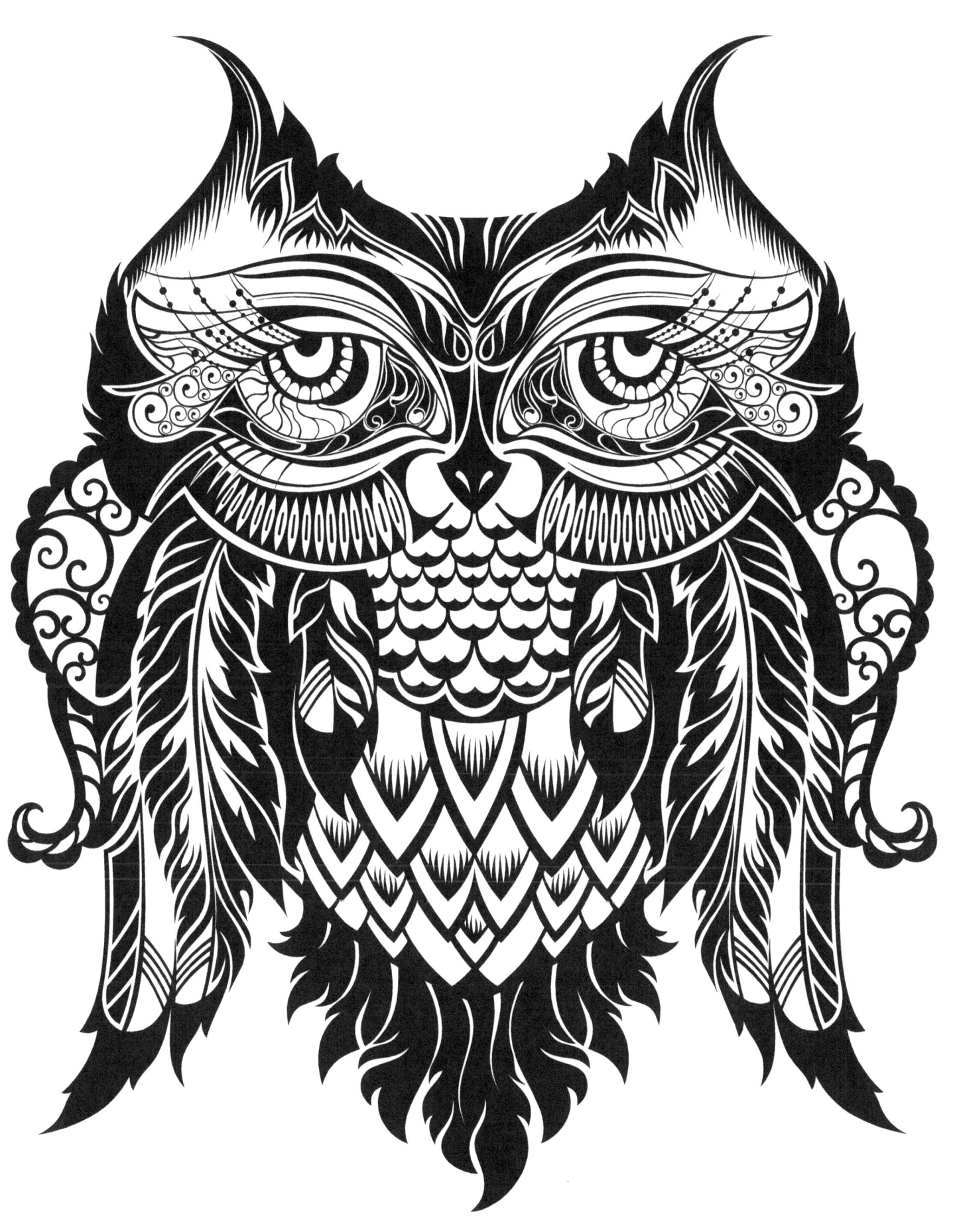

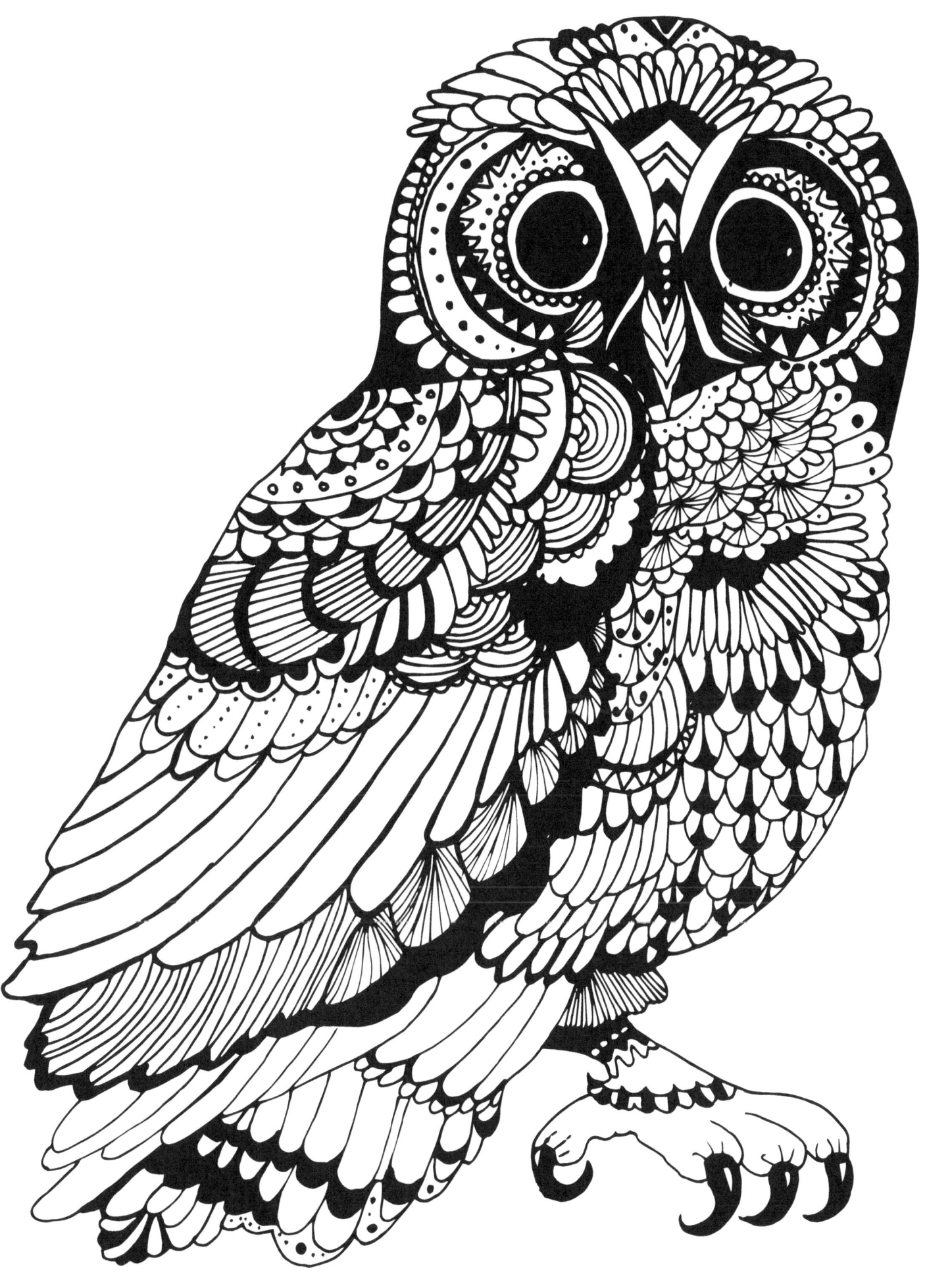

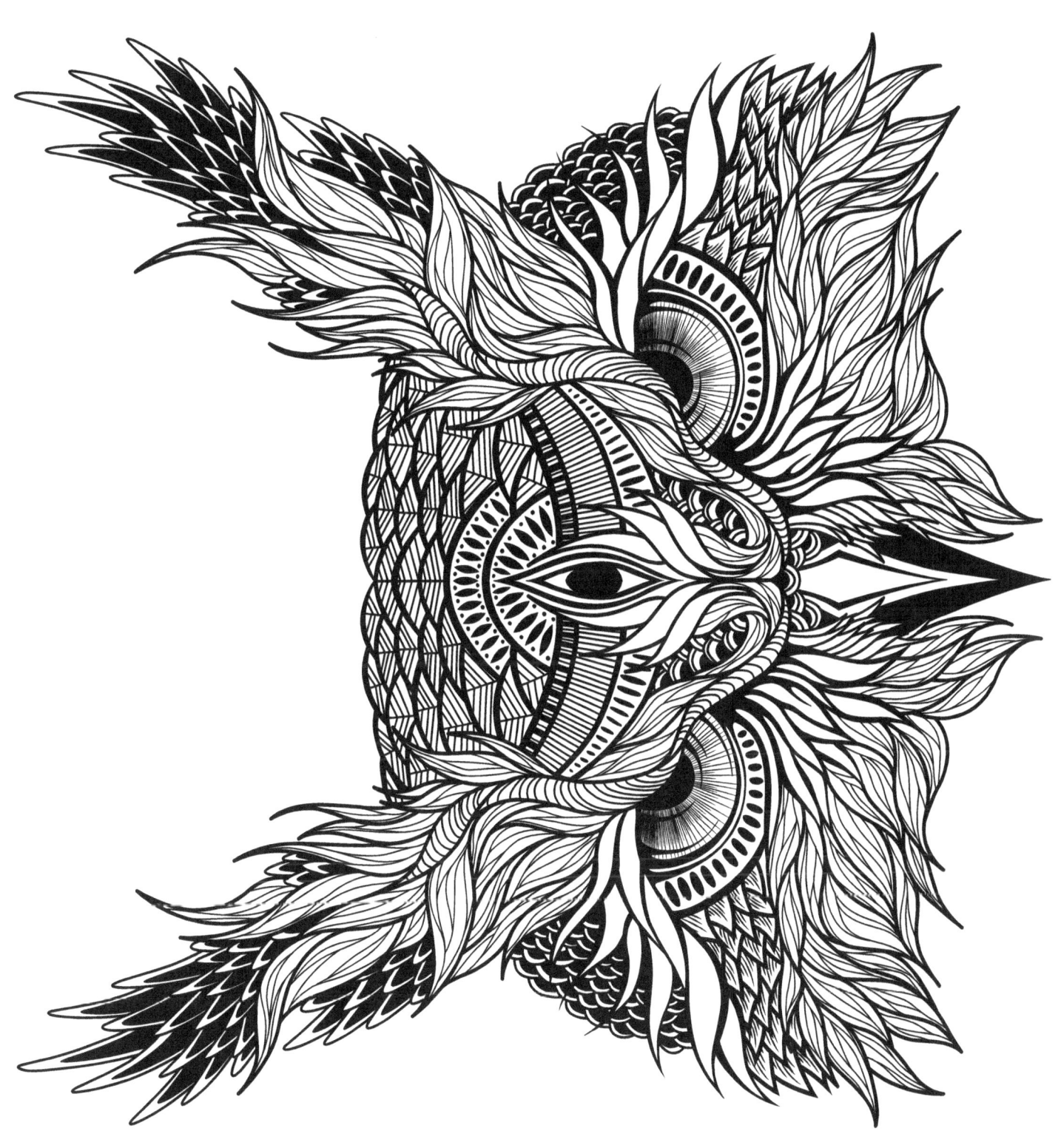

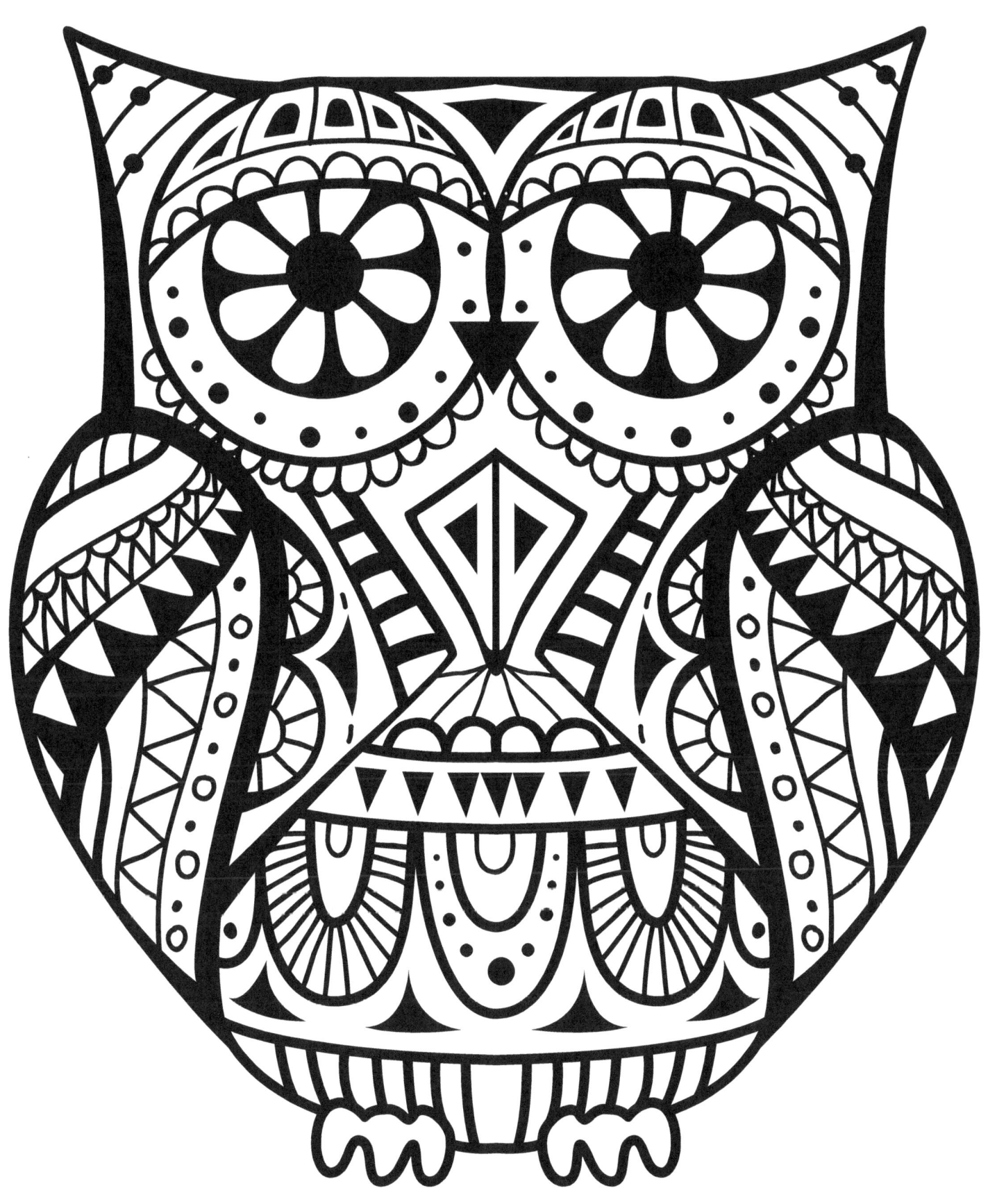

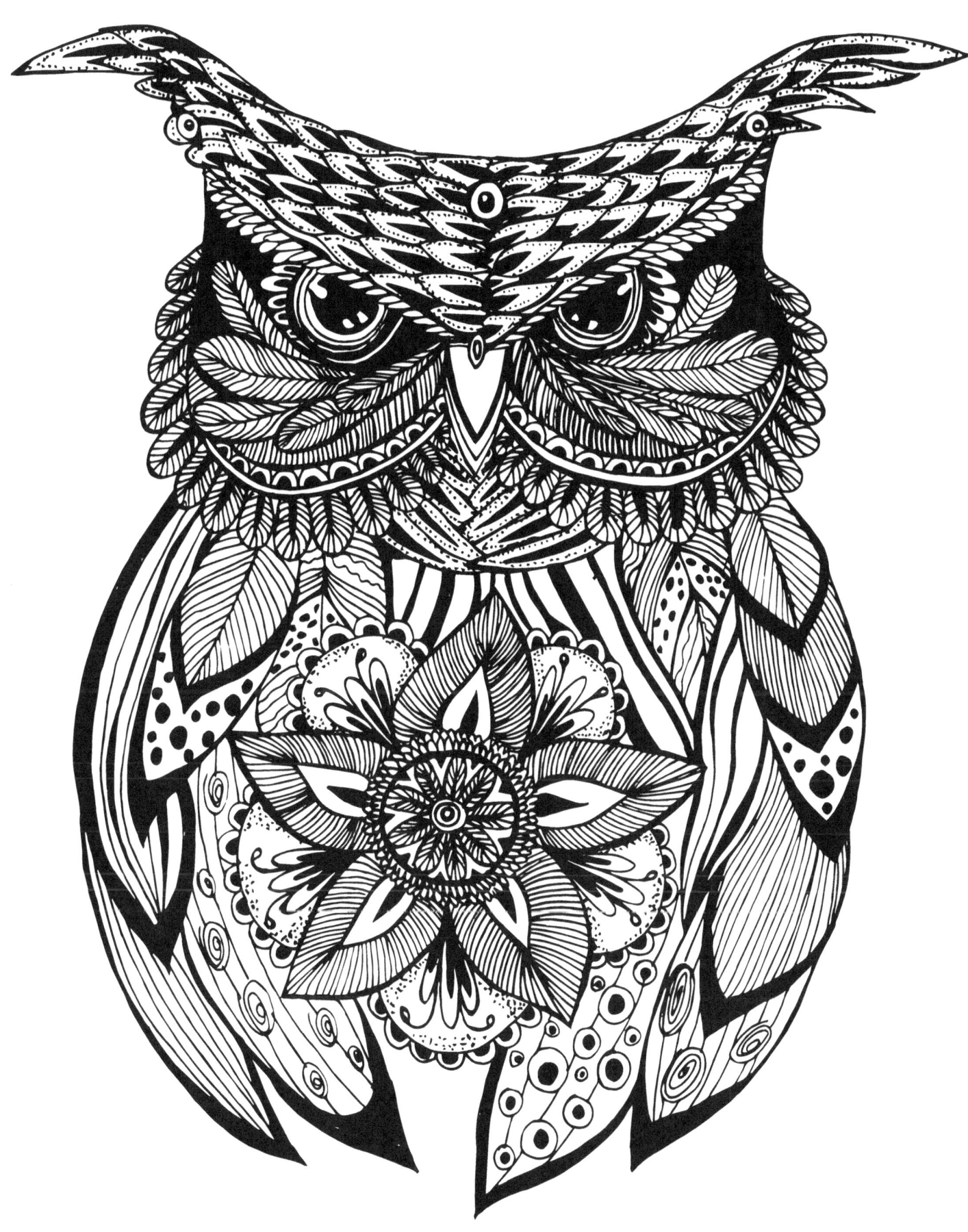

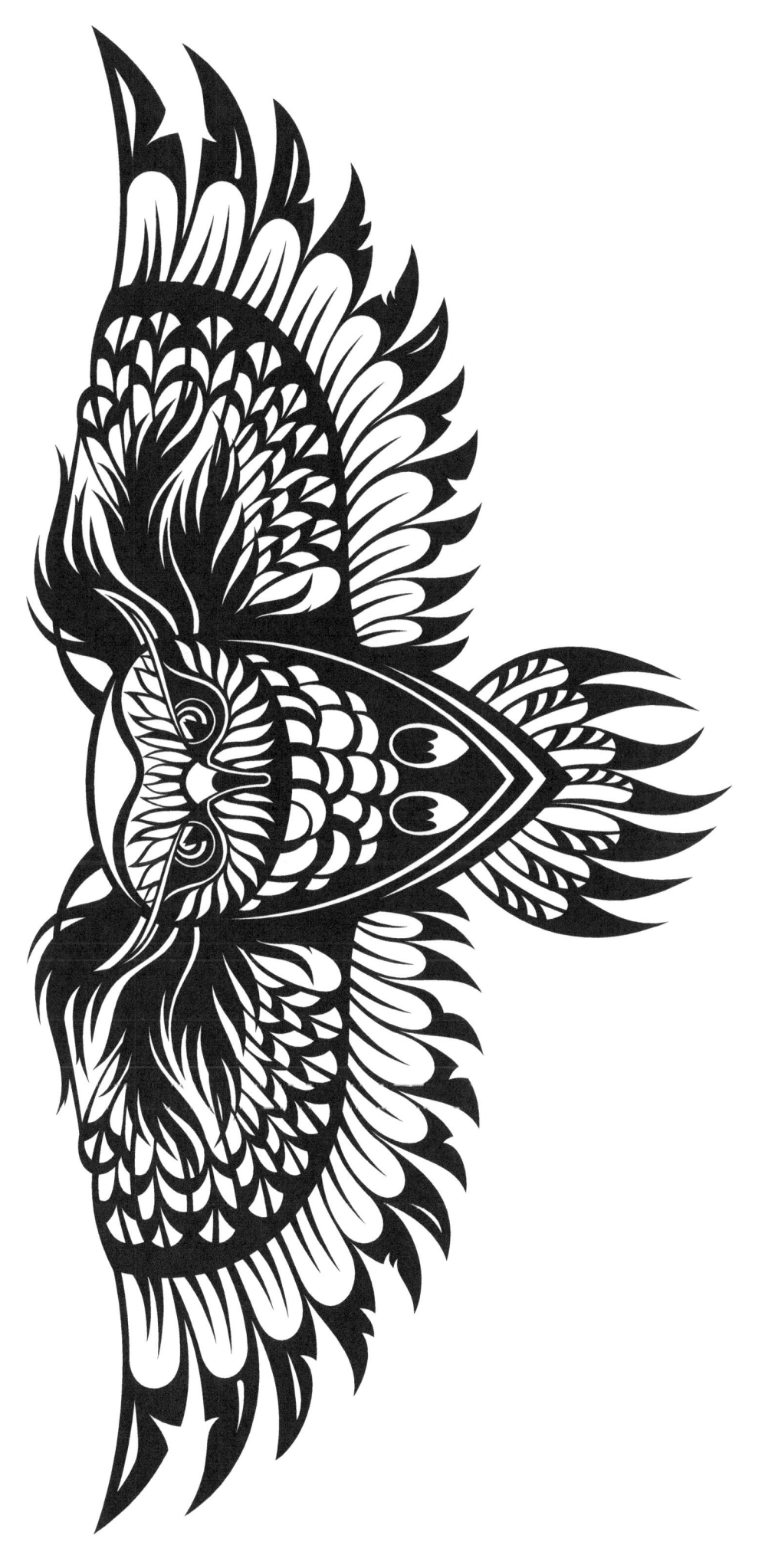

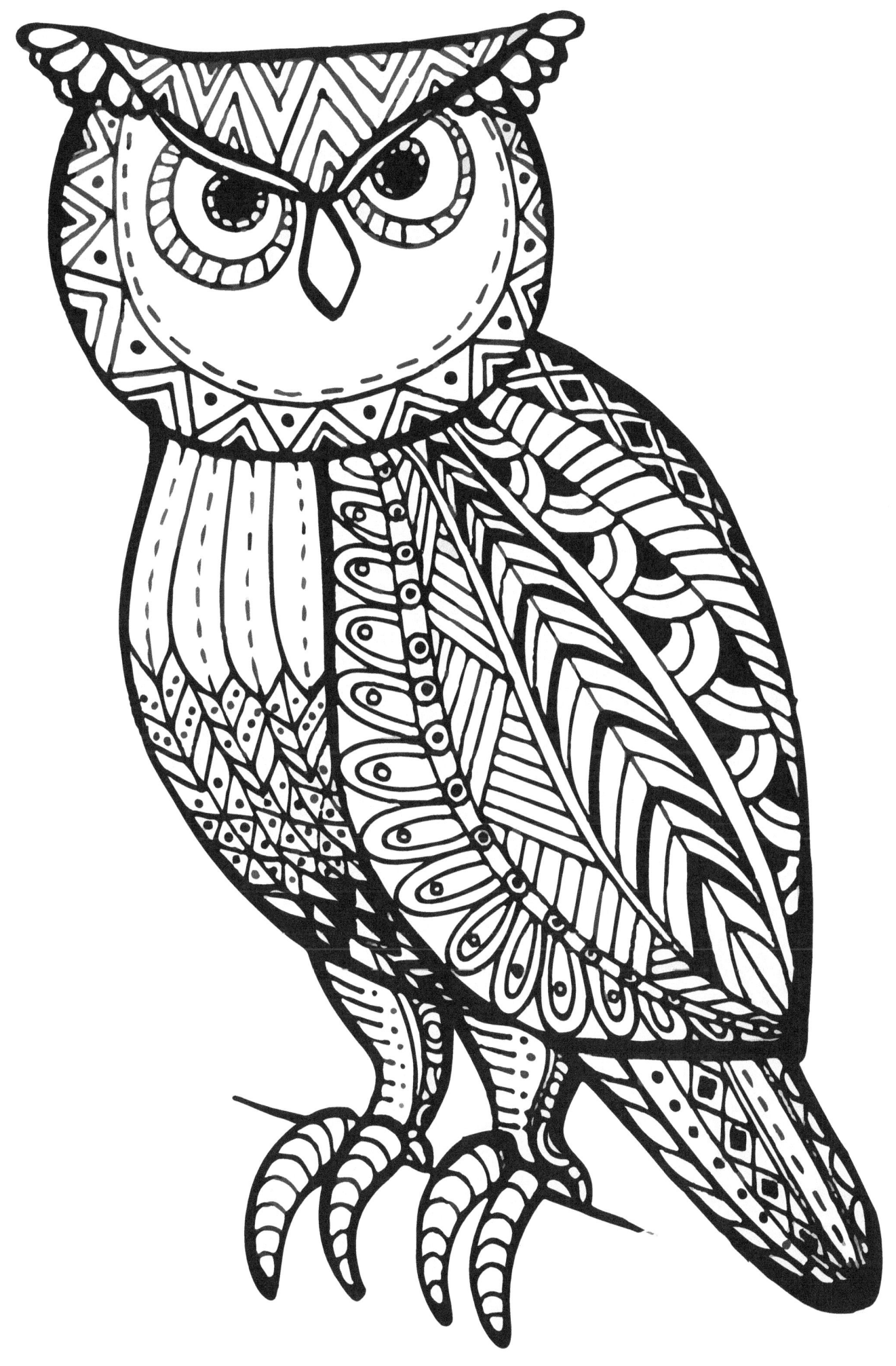

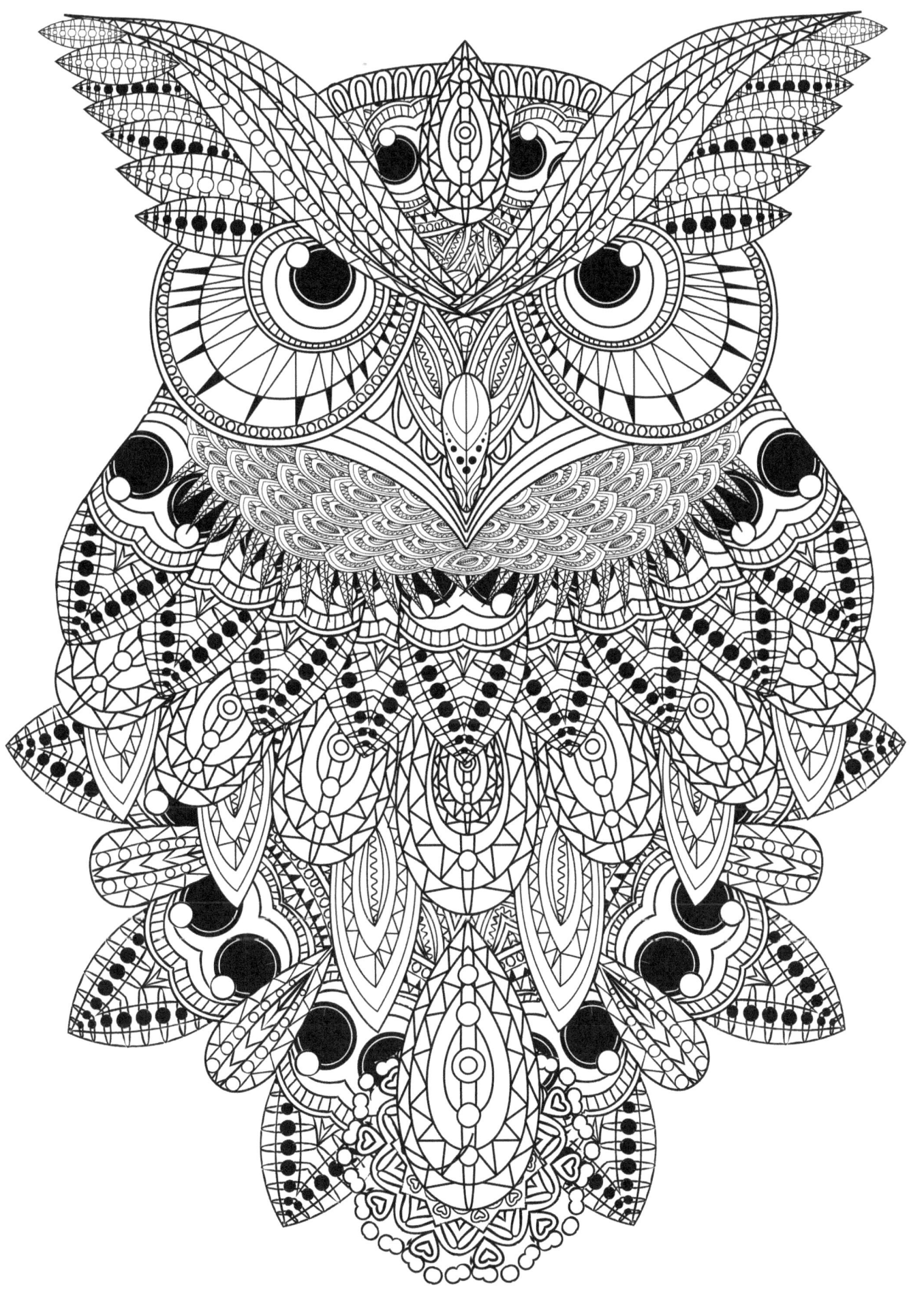

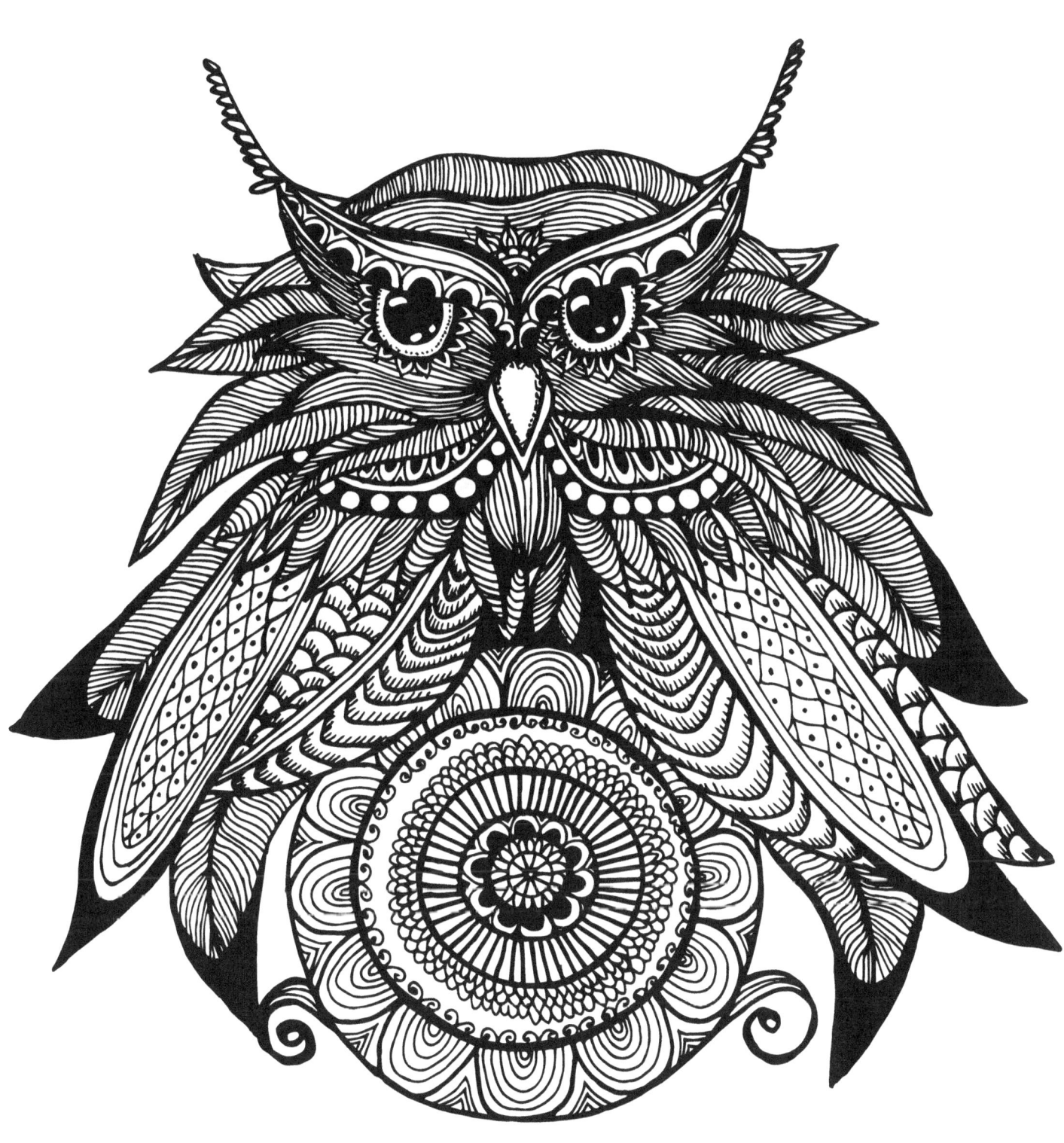

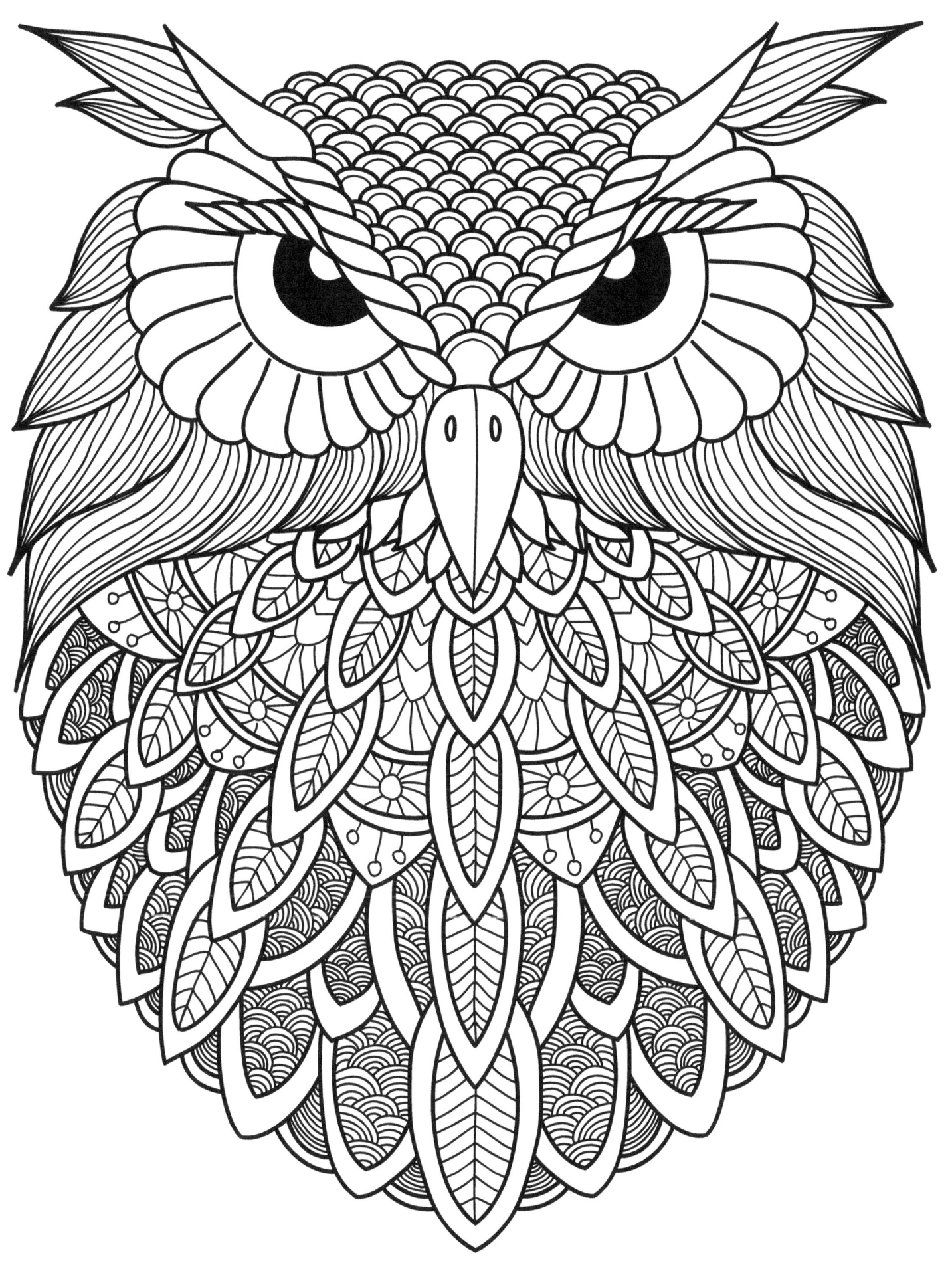

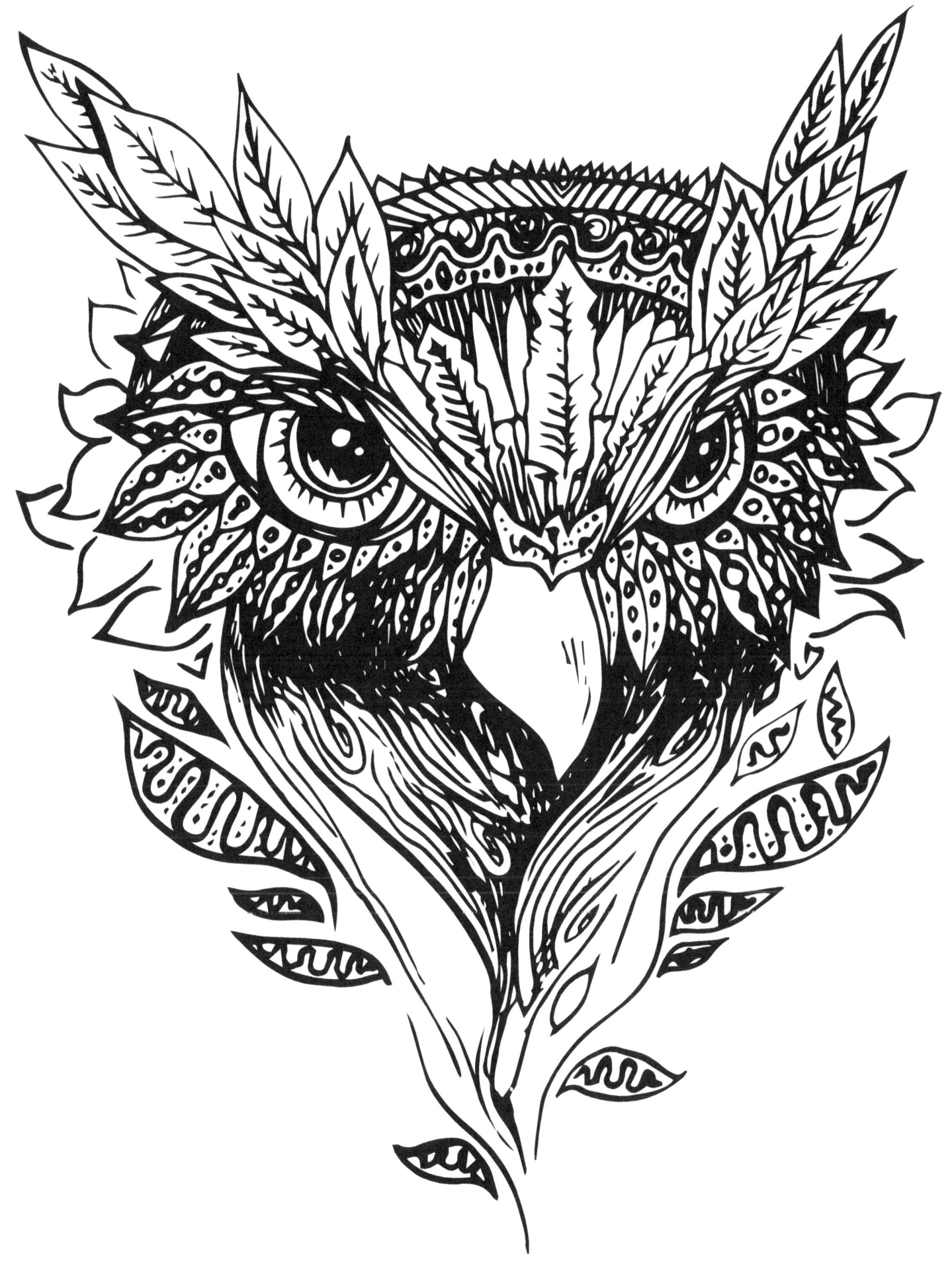

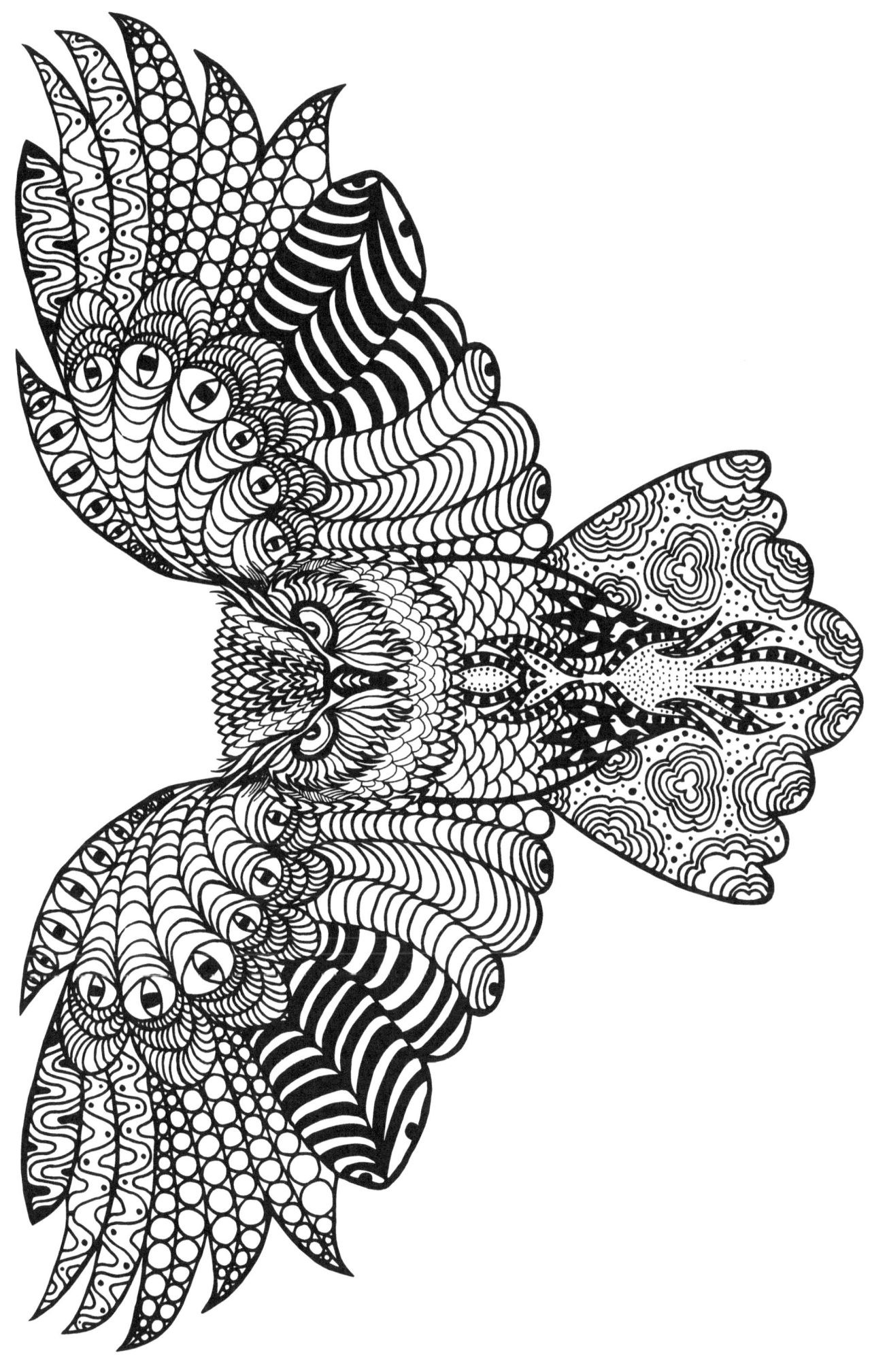

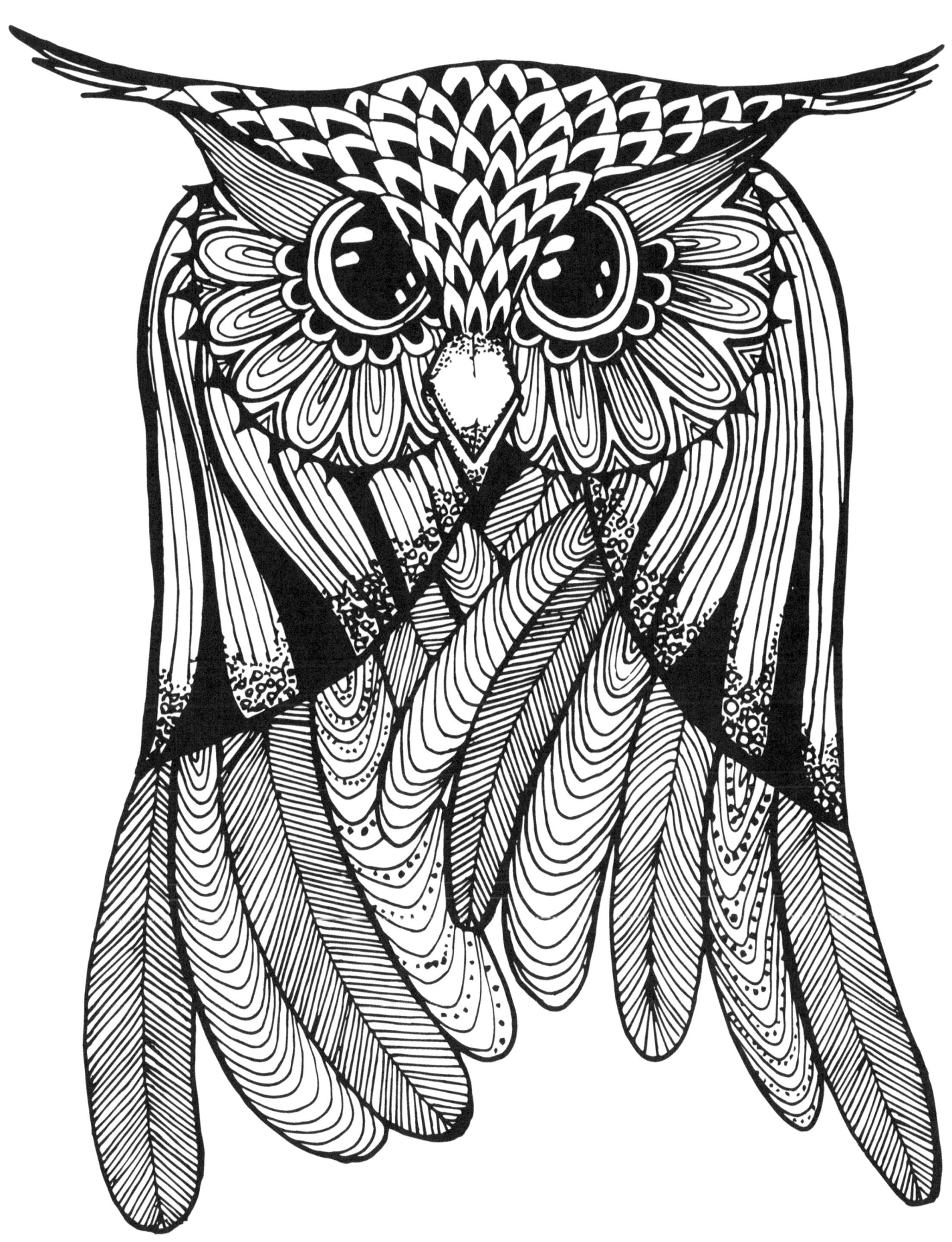

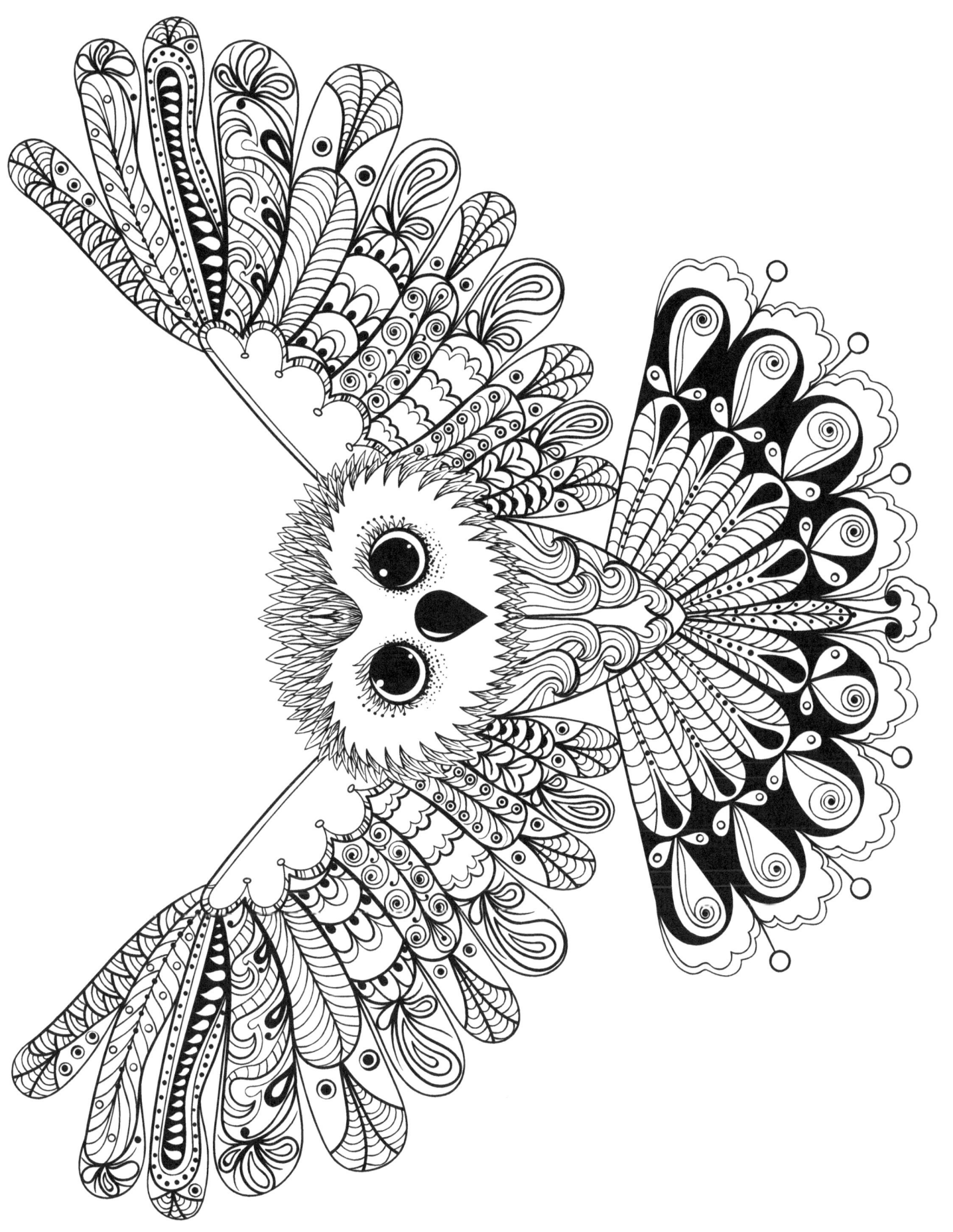

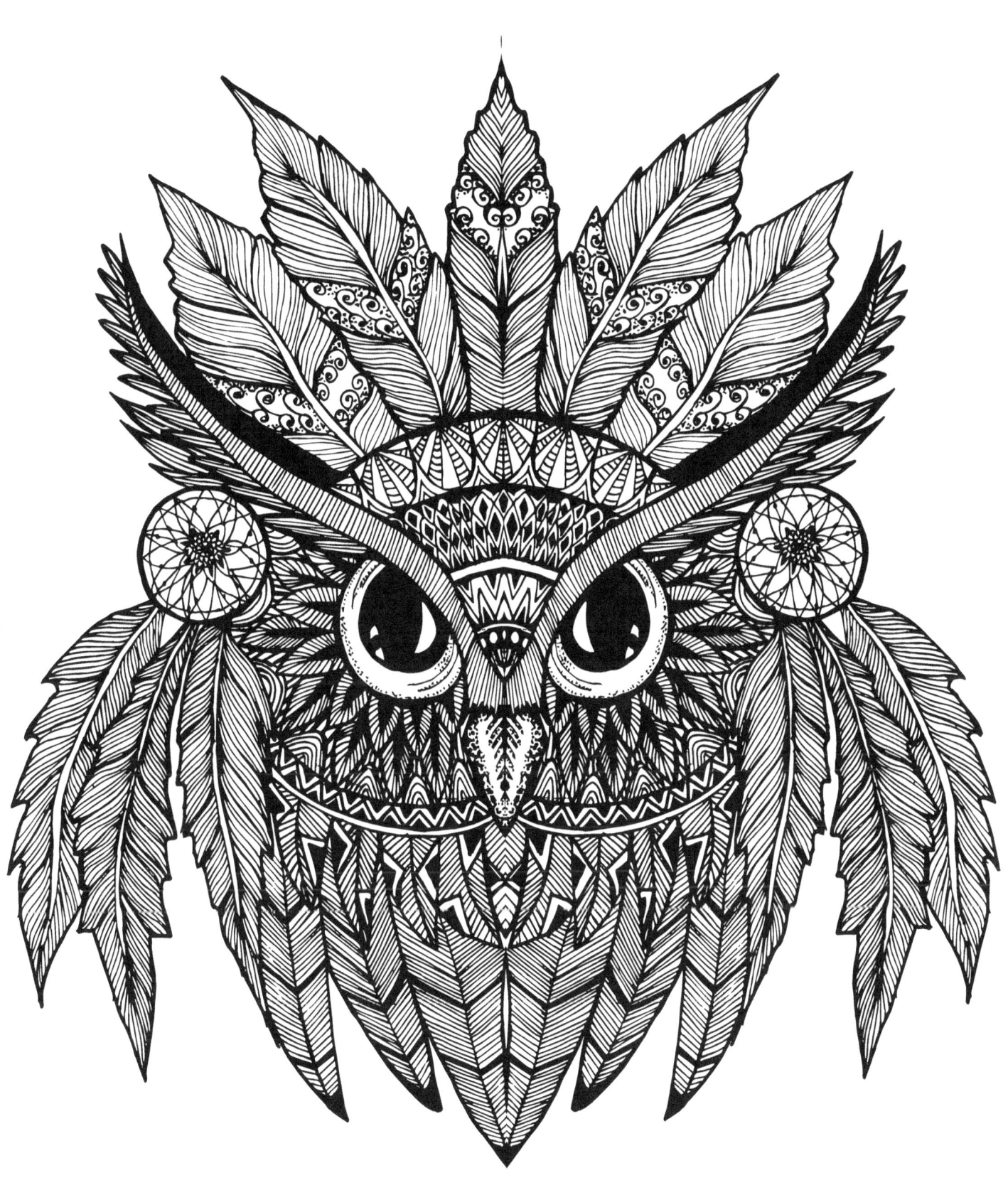

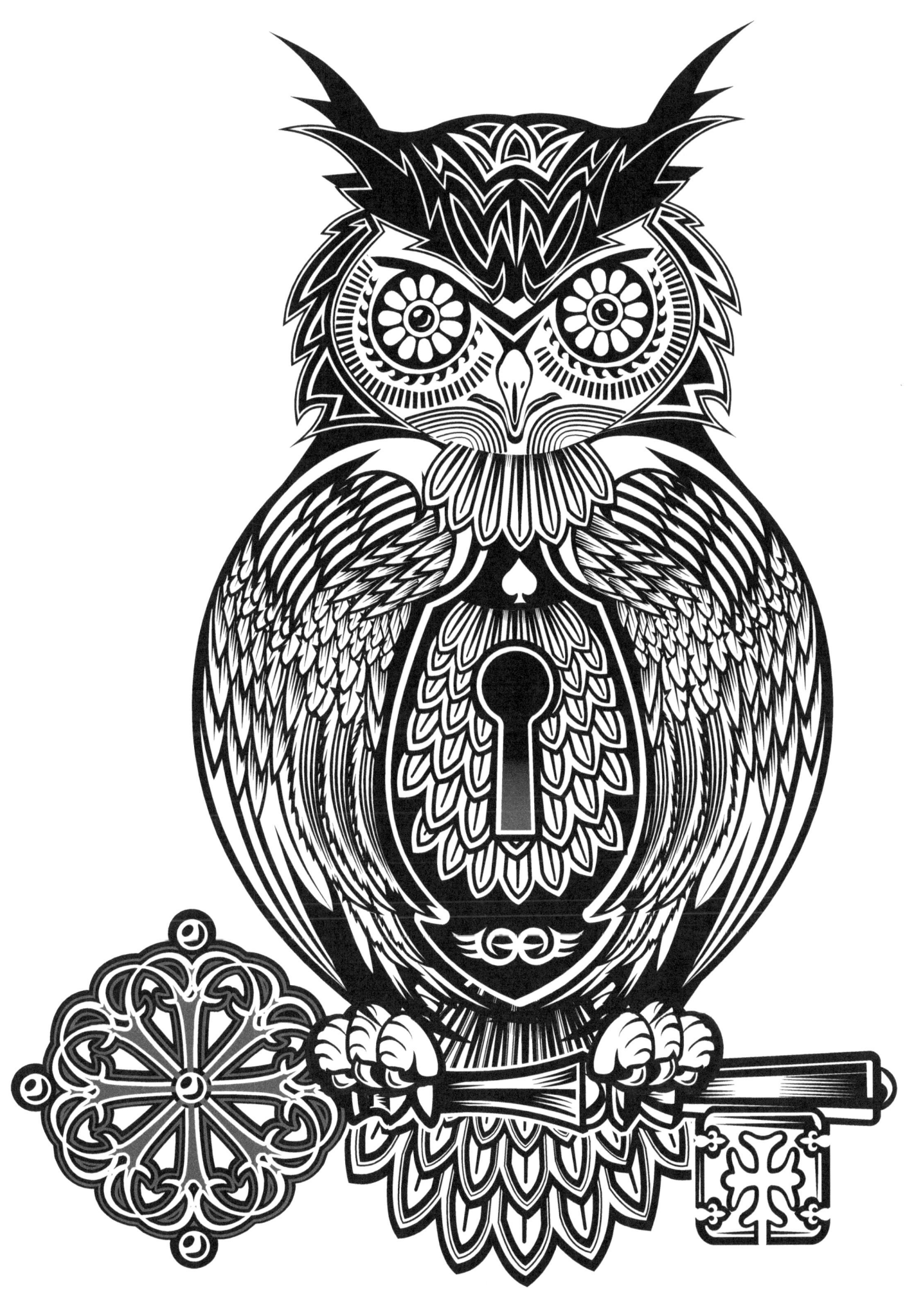

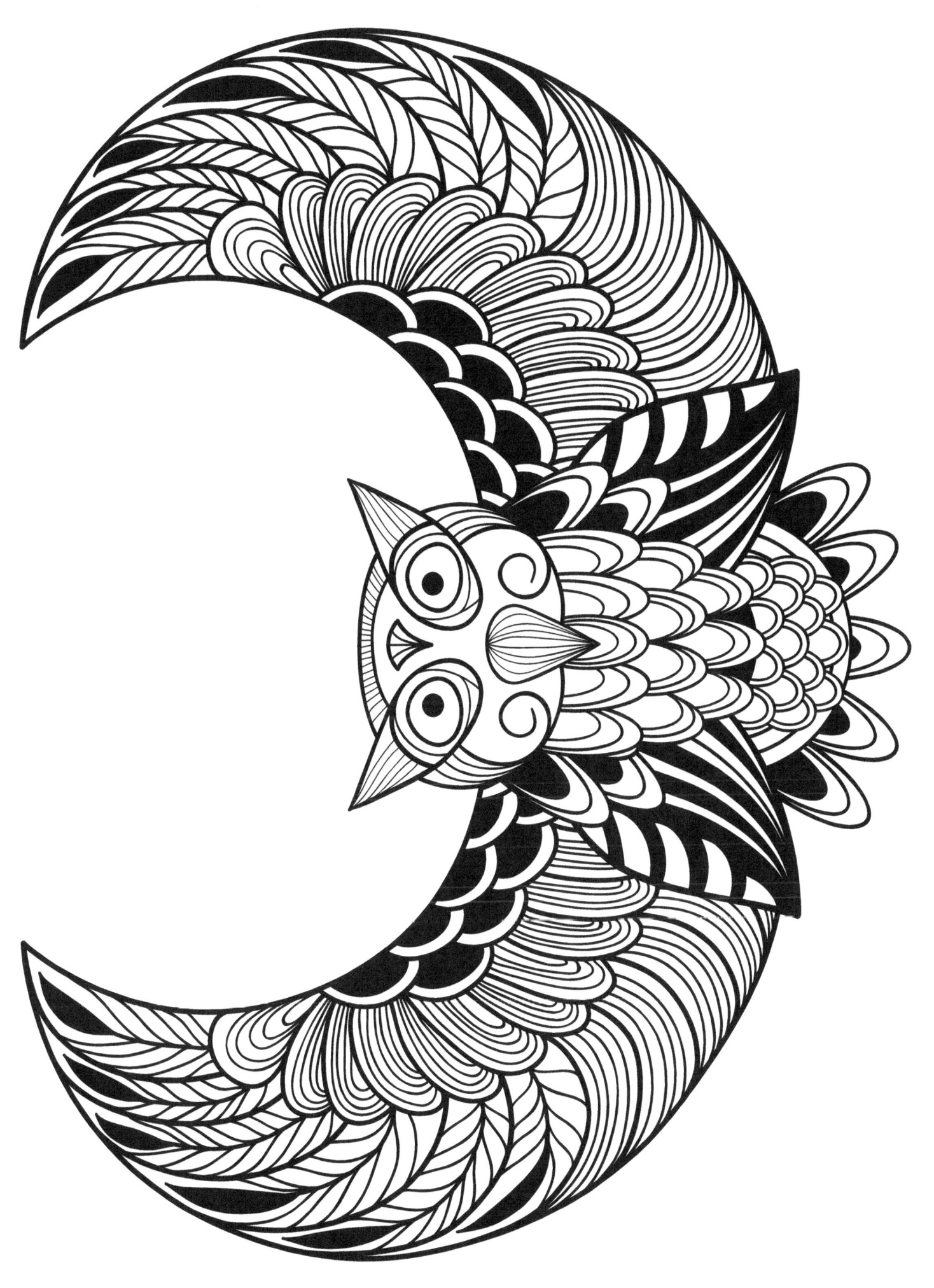

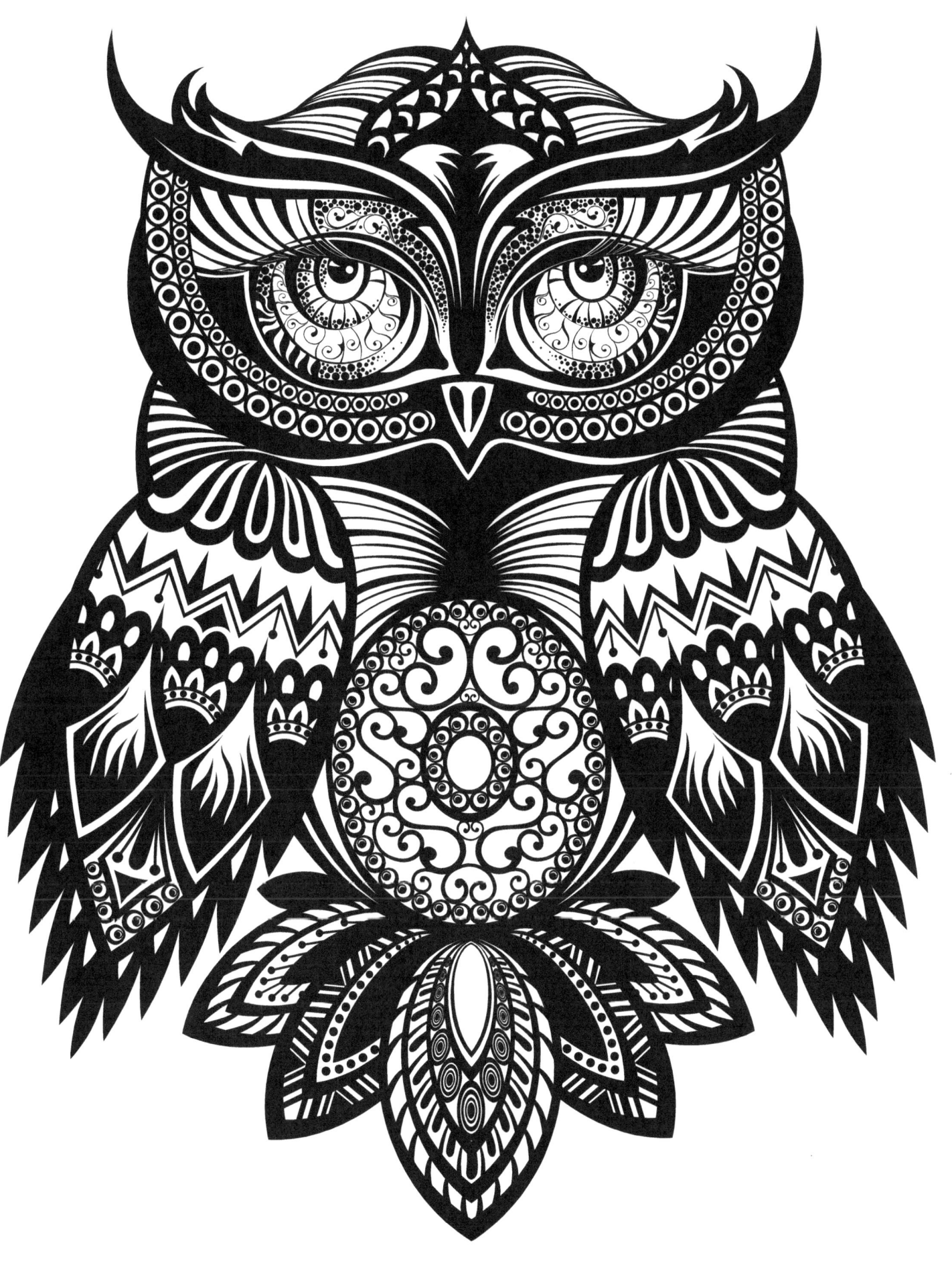

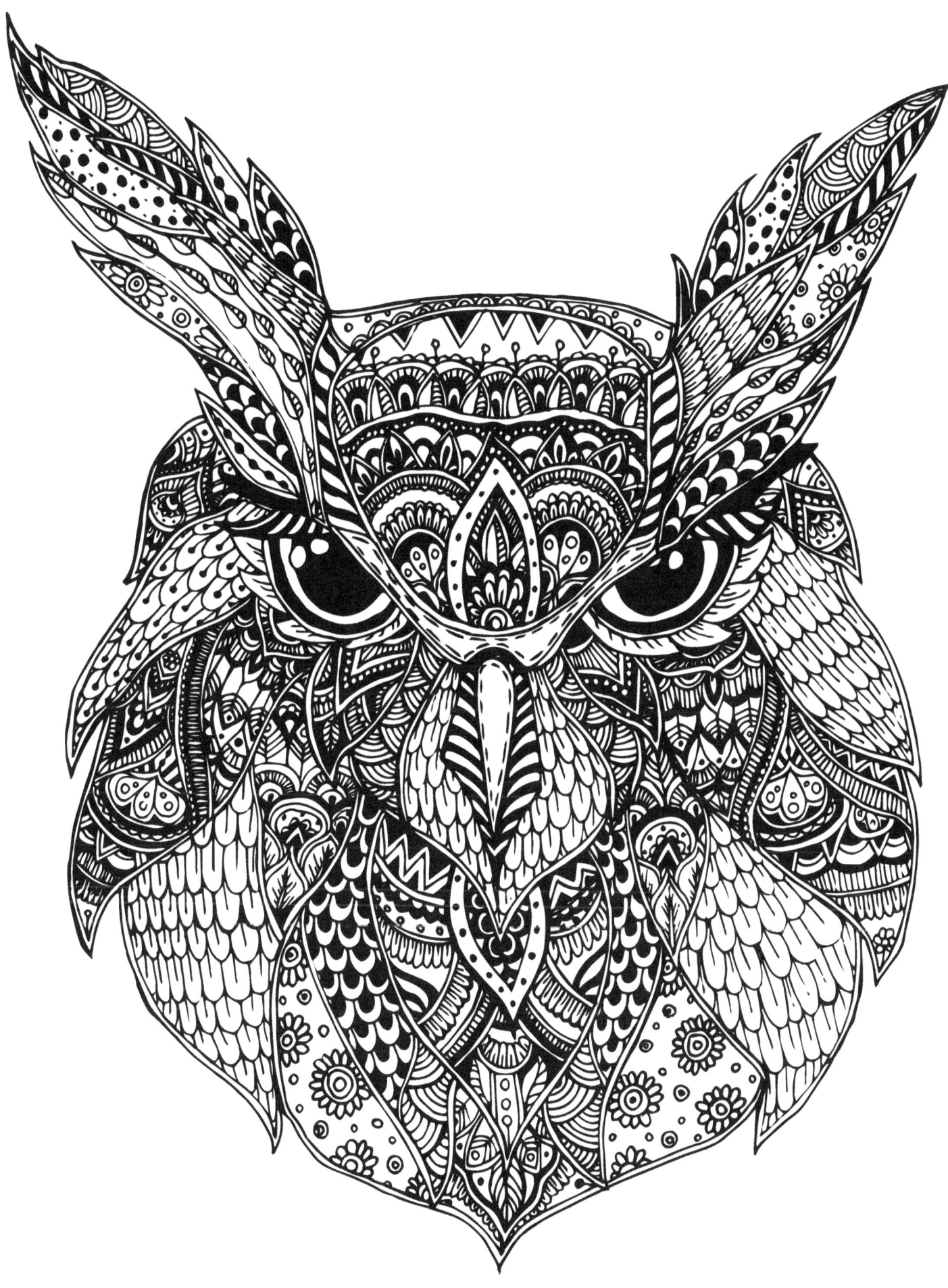

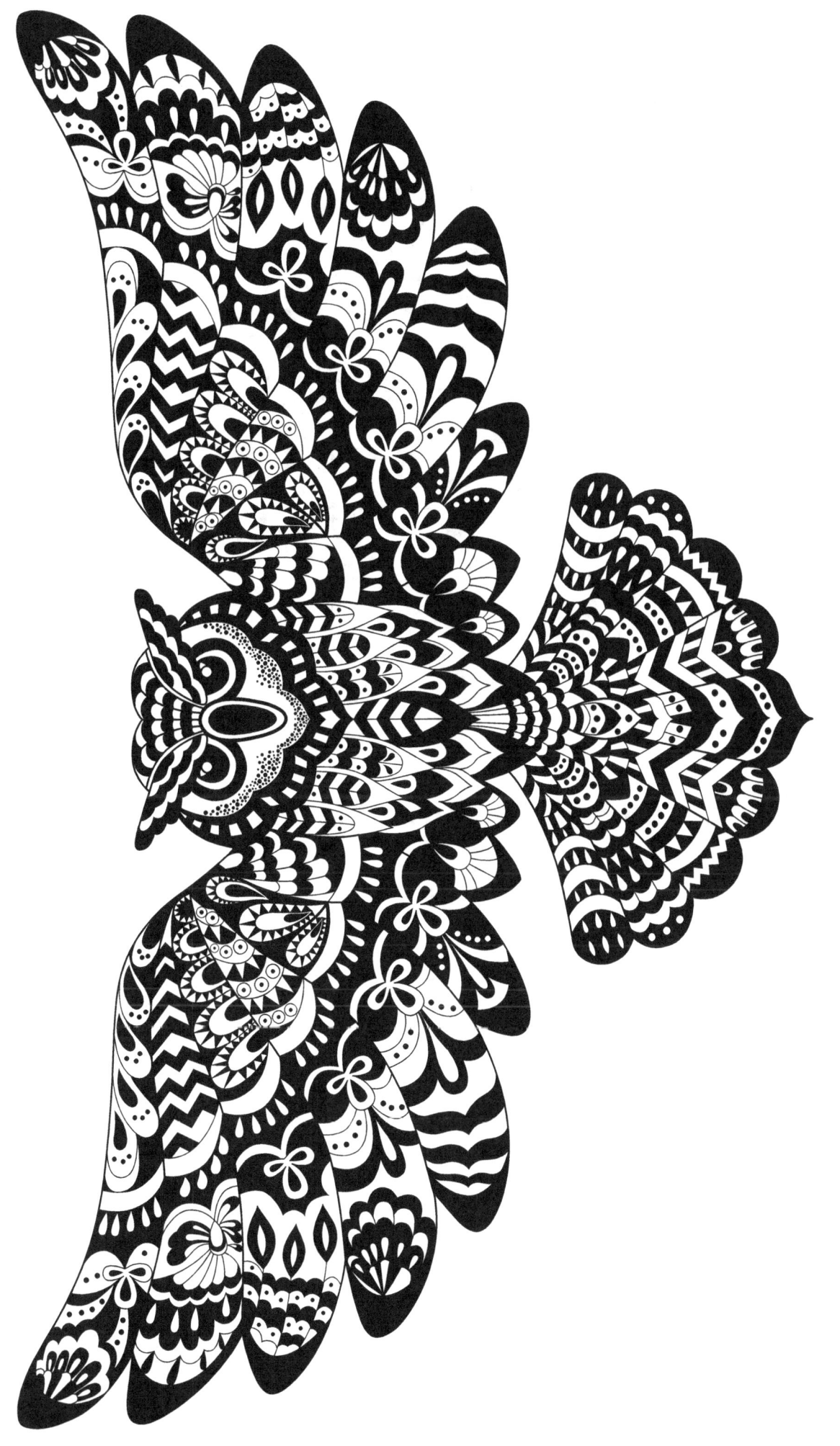

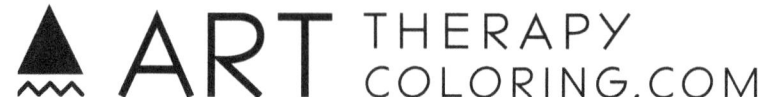

ART THERAPY
COLORING.COM

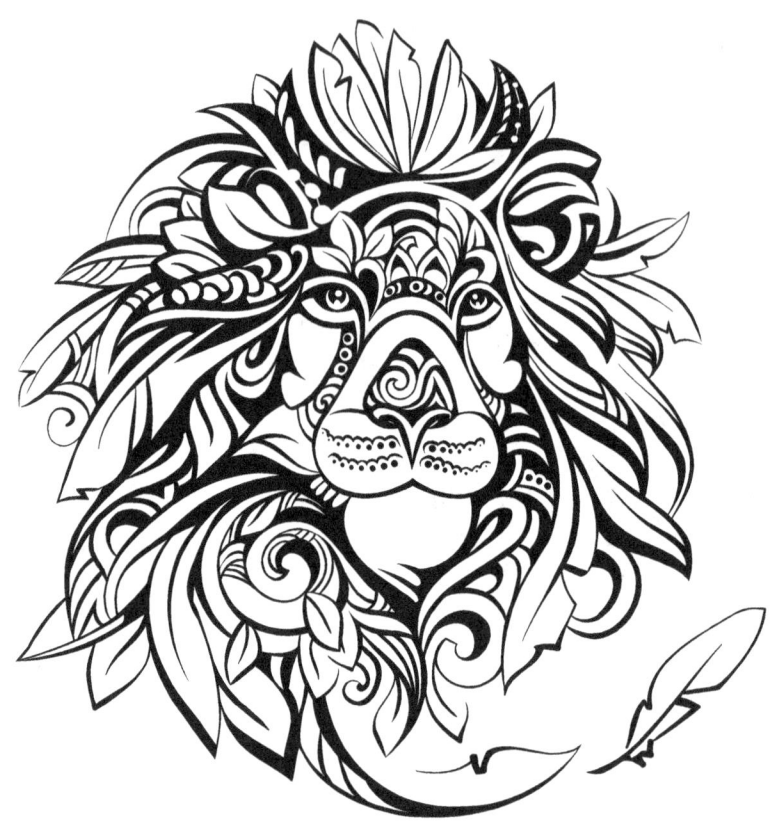

# Did You Enjoy Our Coloring Book?

# We Want To Hear About It!

Help spread the word about our coloring books! The best way to spread the word is through reviews. We know how busy you are, especially with all of that coloring, but we would appreciate it!

# Visit our website at www.arttherapycoloring.com

# Over 200 Art Therapy Coloring Books

See our collection of over 200 Art Therapy Coloring Books for Adults, Men, Women, Seniors, Teens, Kids, Boys, and Girls.

# Coloring Books For Adults

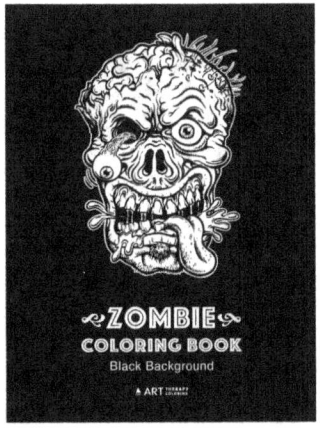

**ZOMBIE**
**COLORING BOOK**
Black Background

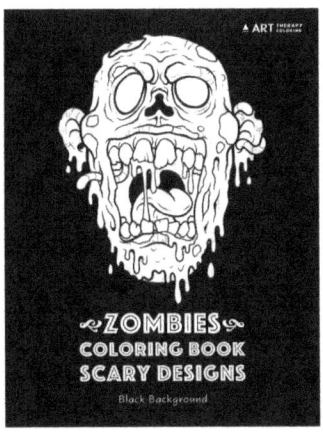

**ZOMBIES**
**COLORING BOOK**
**SCARY DESIGNS**
Black Background

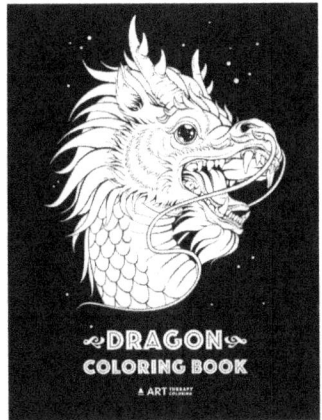

**DRAGON**
**COLORING BOOK**

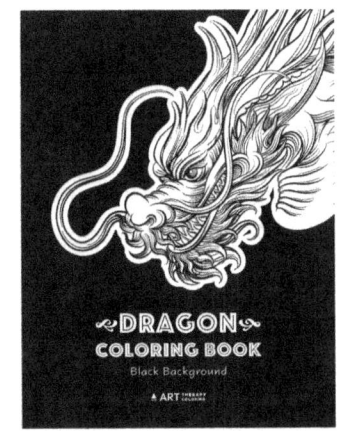

**DRAGON**
**COLORING BOOK**
Black Background

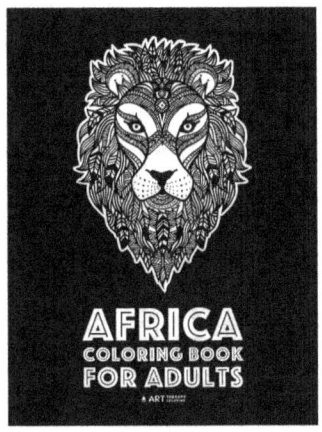

**AFRICA**
**COLORING BOOK**
**FOR ADULTS**

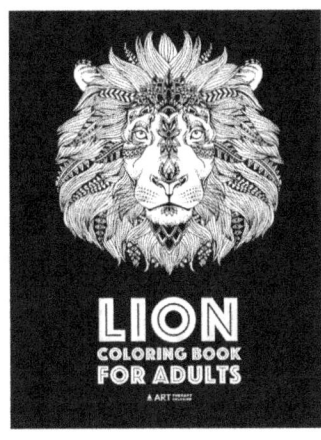

**LION**
**COLORING BOOK**
**FOR ADULTS**

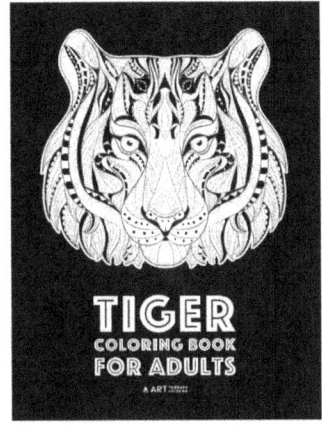

**TIGER**
**COLORING BOOK**
**FOR ADULTS**

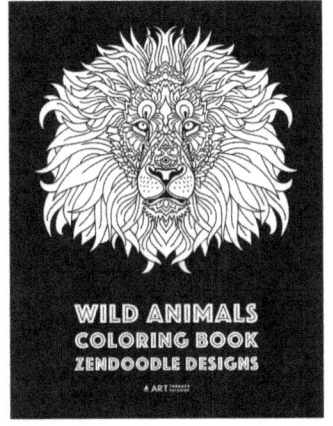

**WILD ANIMALS**
**COLORING BOOK**
**ZENDOODLE DESIGNS**

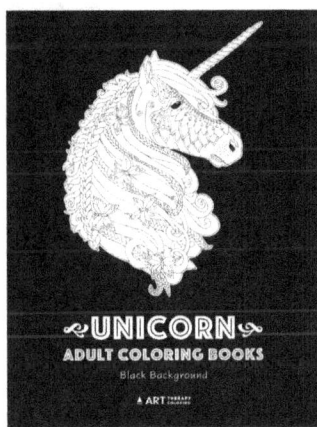

**UNICORN**
**ADULT COLORING BOOKS**
Black Background

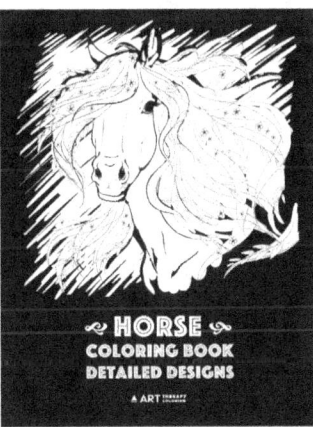

**HORSE**
**COLORING BOOK**
**DETAILED DESIGNS**

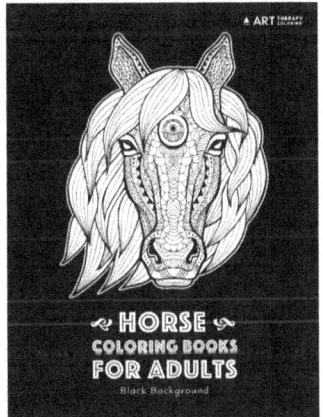

**HORSE**
**COLORING BOOKS**
**FOR ADULTS**
Black Background

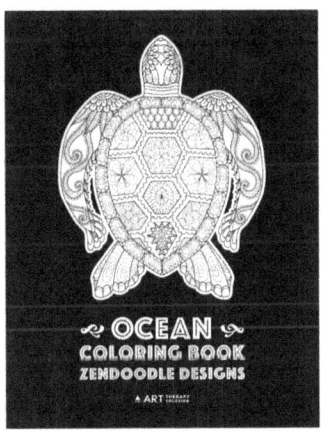

**OCEAN**
**COLORING BOOK**
**ZENDOODLE DESIGNS**

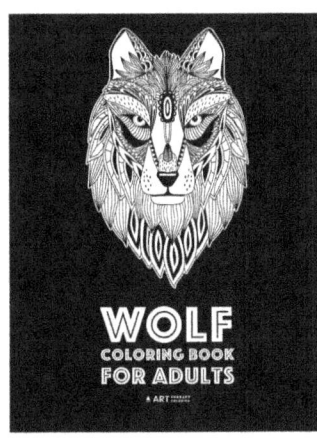

**WOLF**
**COLORING BOOK**
**FOR ADULTS**

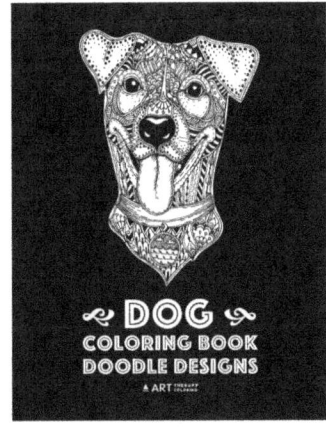

**DOG**
**COLORING BOOK**
**DOODLE DESIGNS**

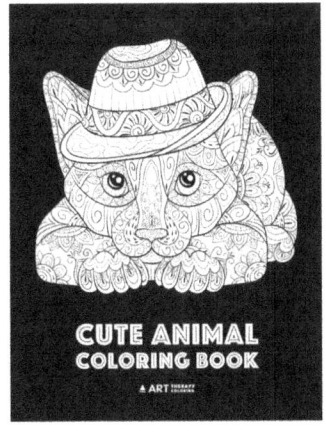

**CUTE ANIMAL**
**COLORING BOOK**

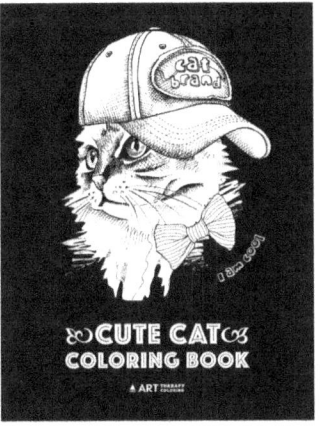

**CUTE CAT**
**COLORING BOOK**

# Coloring Books For Adults

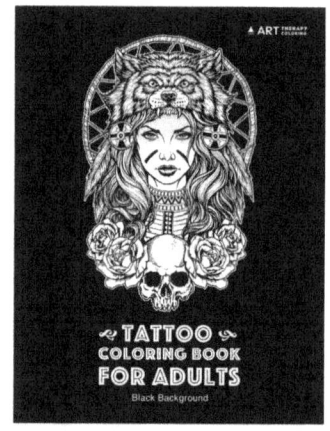

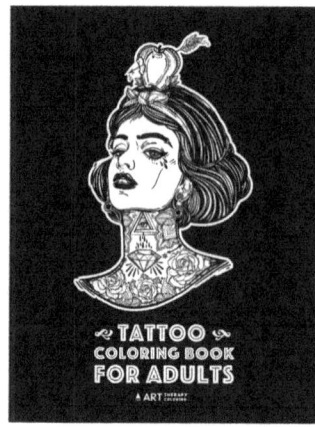

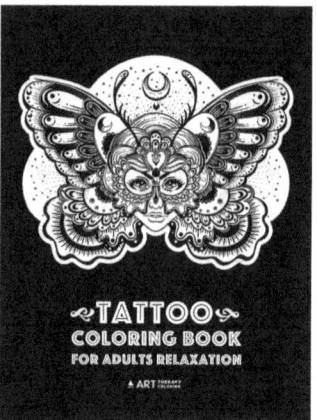

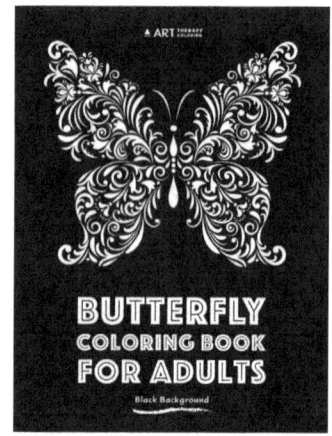

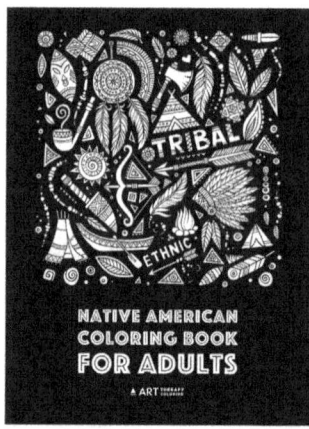

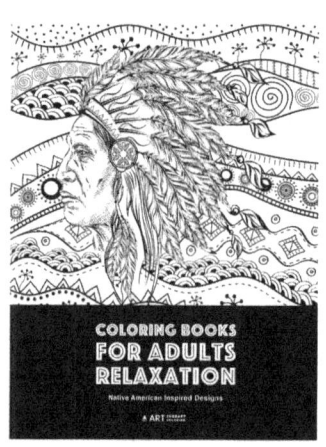

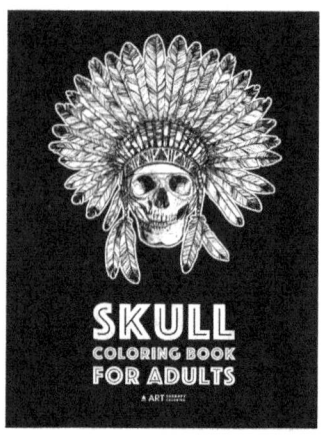

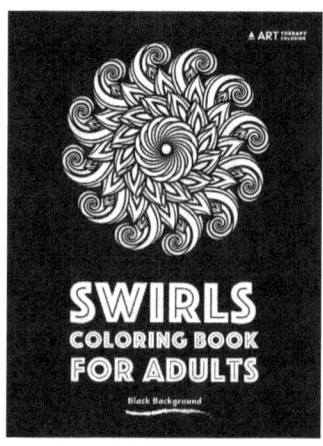

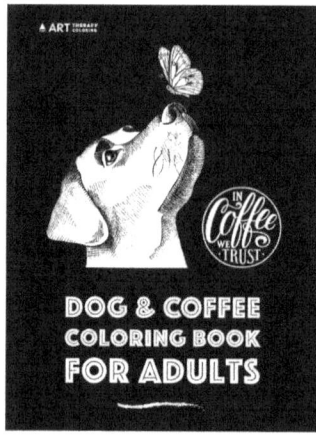

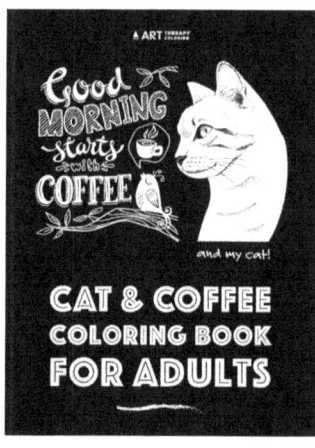

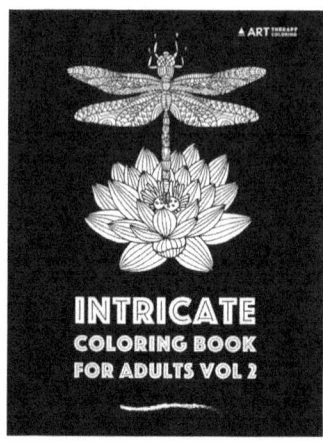

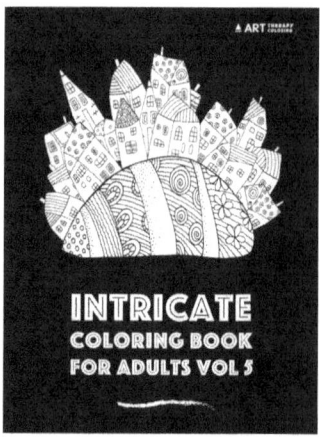

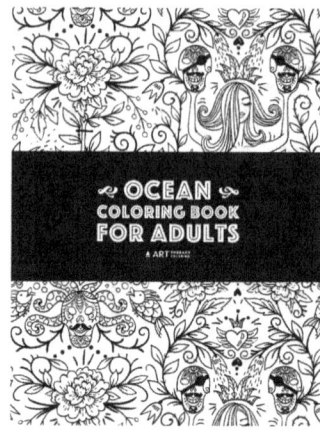

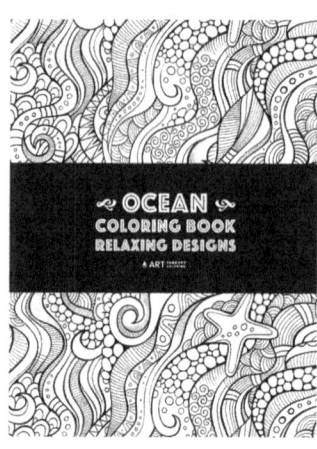

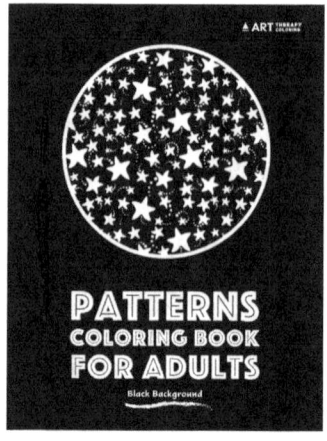

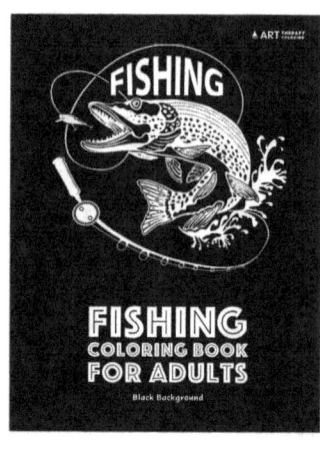

# Coloring Books For Adults

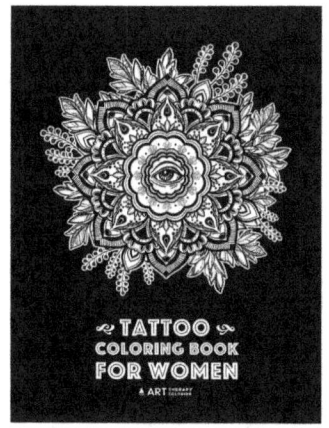

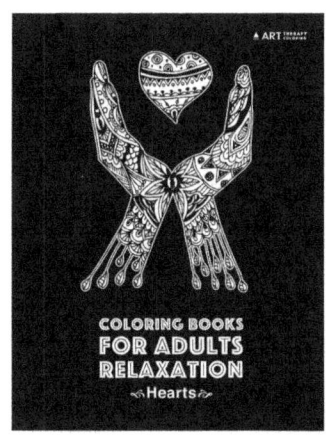

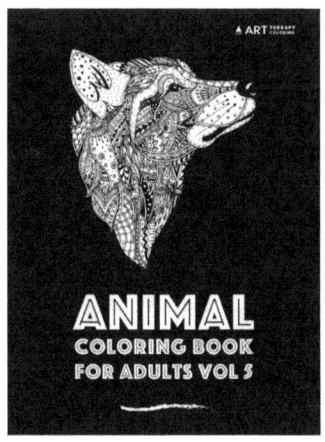

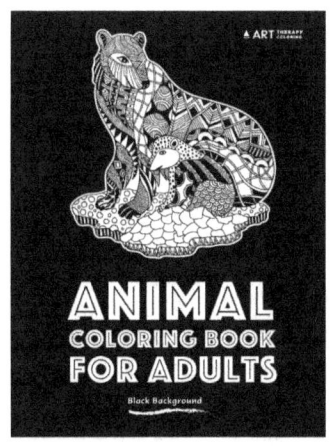

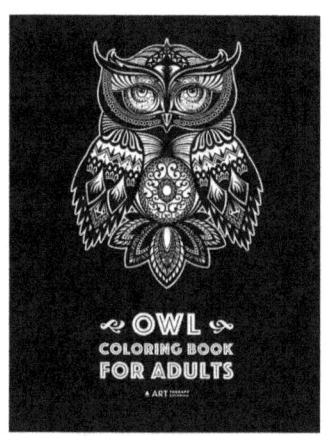

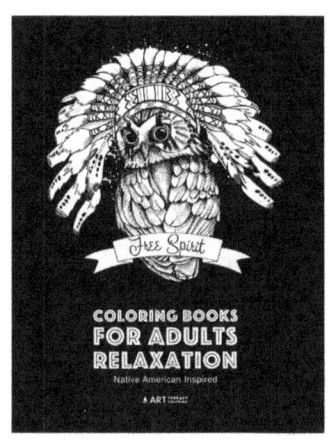

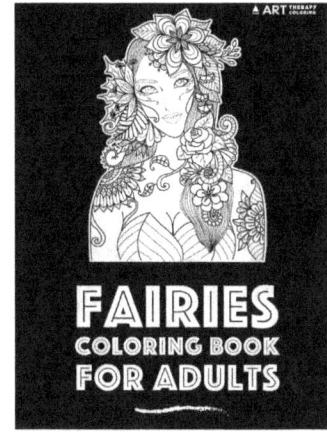

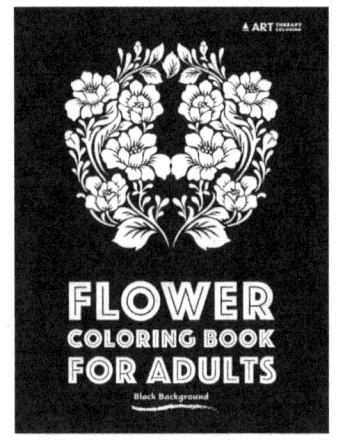

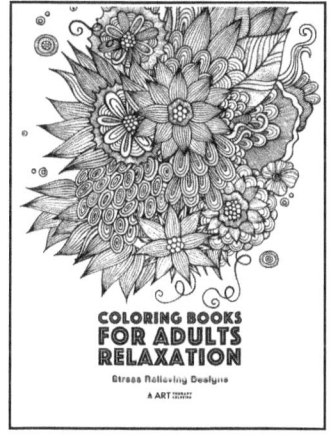

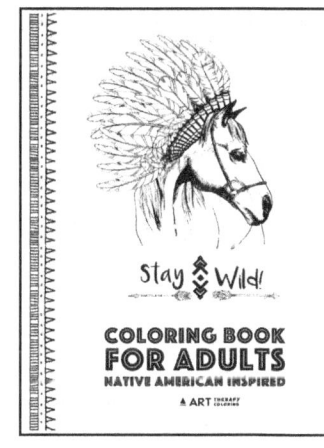

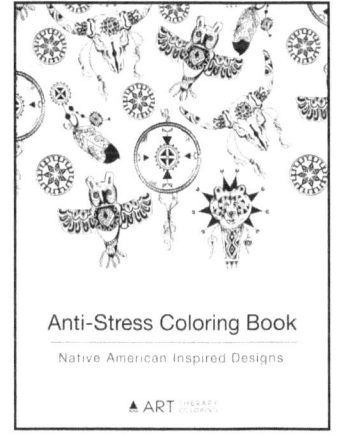

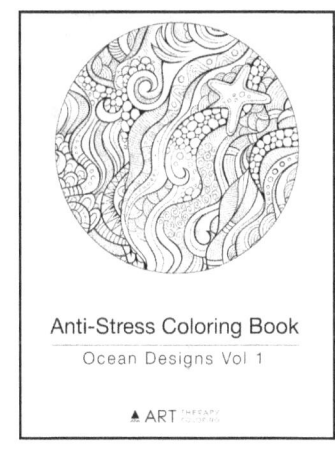

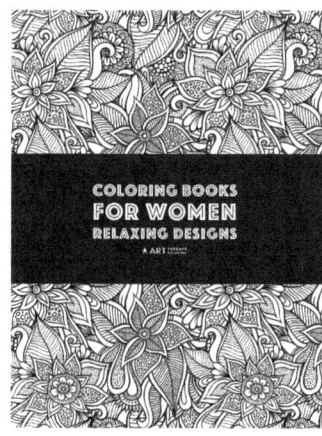

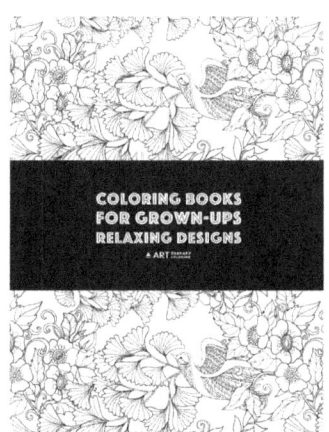

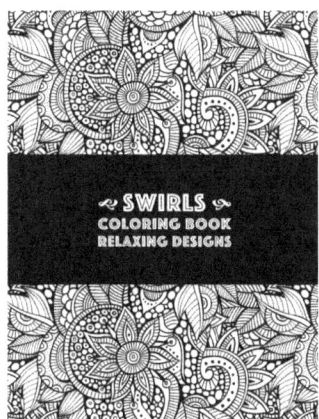

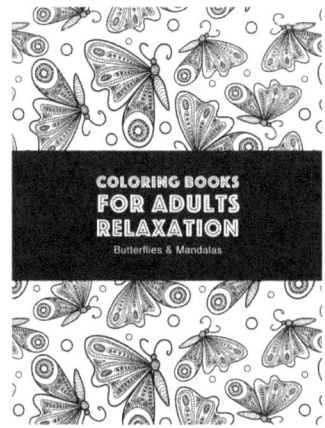

# Coloring Books For Men

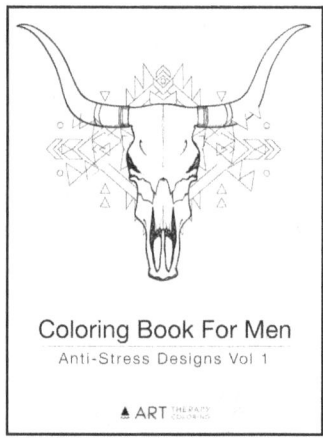

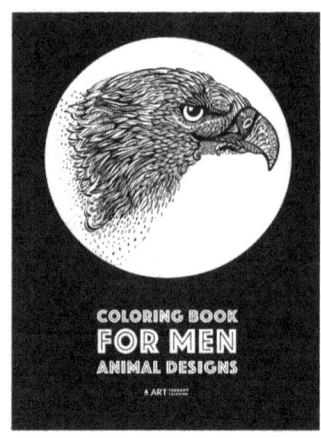

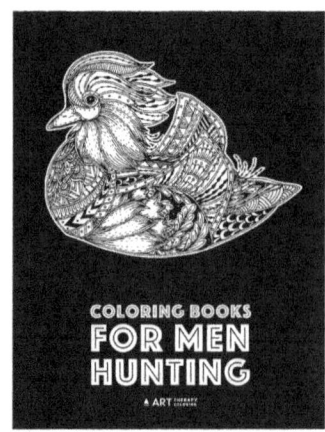

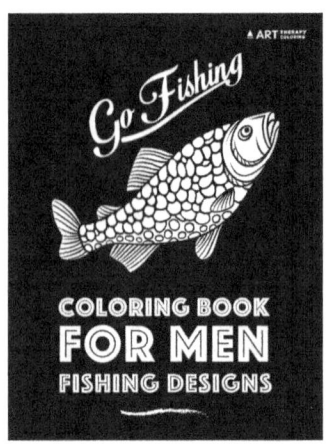

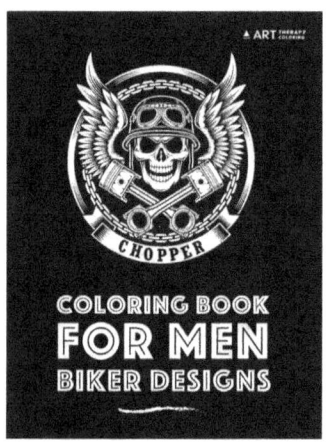

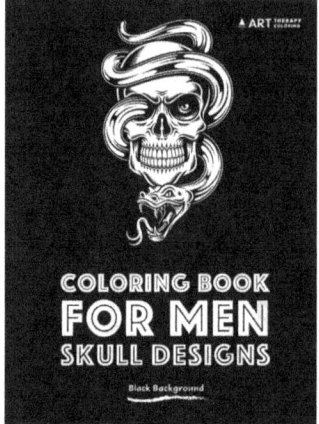

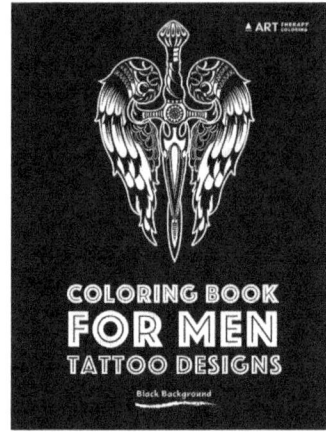

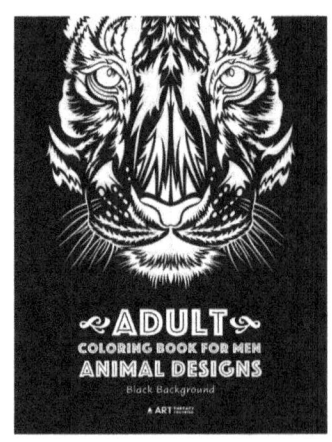

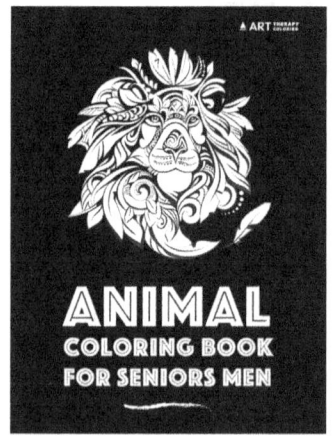

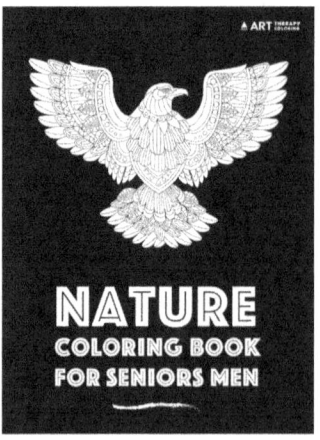

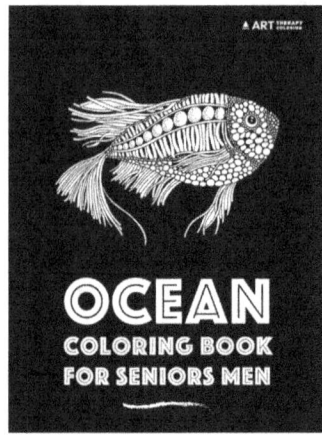

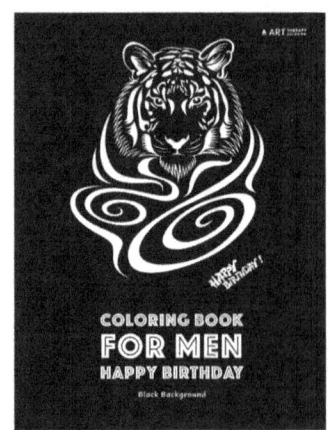

# Coloring Books For Seniors

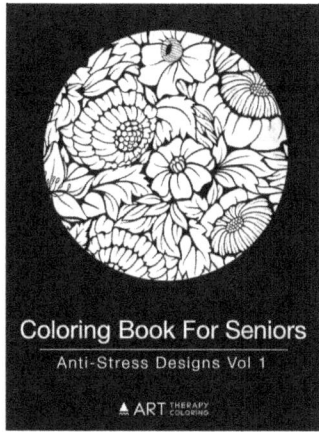

Coloring Book For Seniors
Anti-Stress Designs Vol 1

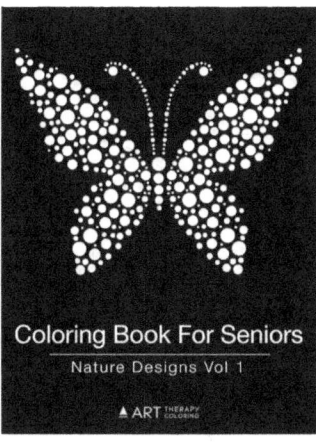

Coloring Book For Seniors
Nature Designs Vol 1

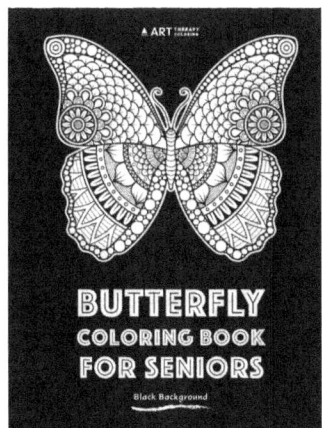

BUTTERFLY
COLORING BOOK
FOR SENIORS
Black Background

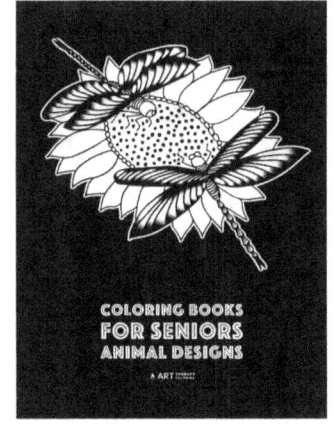

COLORING BOOKS
FOR SENIORS
ANIMAL DESIGNS

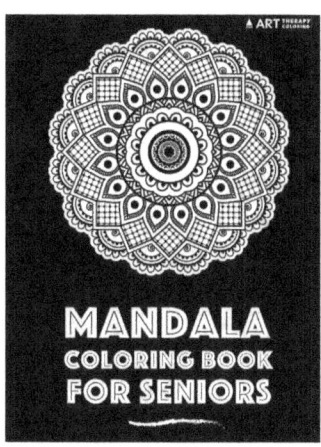

MANDALA
COLORING BOOK
FOR SENIORS

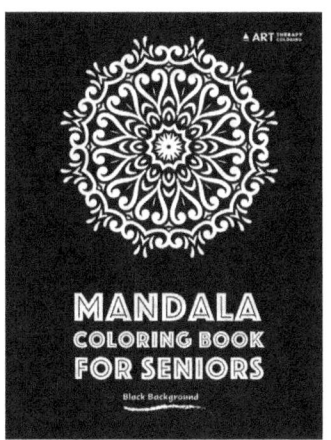

MANDALA
COLORING BOOK
FOR SENIORS
Black Background

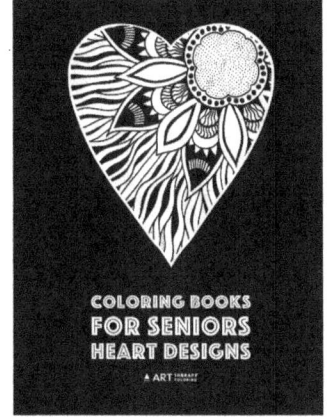

COLORING BOOKS
FOR SENIORS
HEART DESIGNS

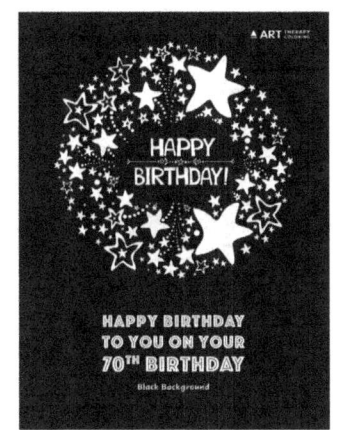

HAPPY BIRTHDAY
TO YOU ON YOUR
70TH BIRTHDAY
Black Background

COLORING BOOKS
FOR SENIORS
SWIRL DESIGNS
Black Background

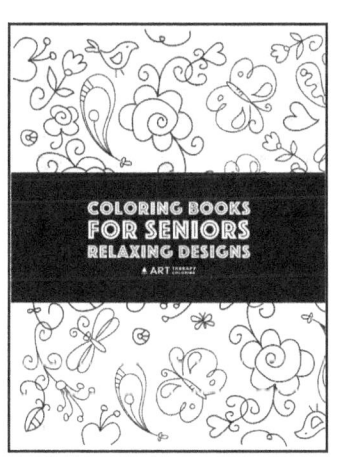

COLORING BOOKS
FOR SENIORS
RELAXING DESIGNS

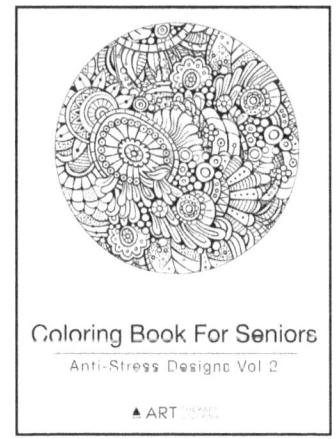

Coloring Book For Seniors
Anti-Stress Designs Vol 2

Coloring Book For Seniors
Anti-Stress Designs Vol 3

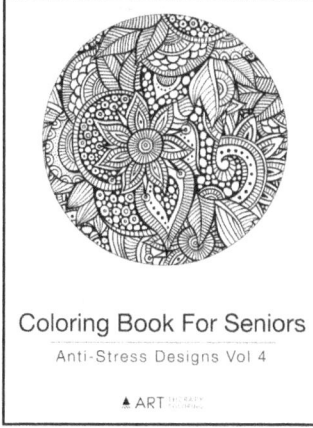

Coloring Book For Seniors
Anti-Stress Designs Vol 4

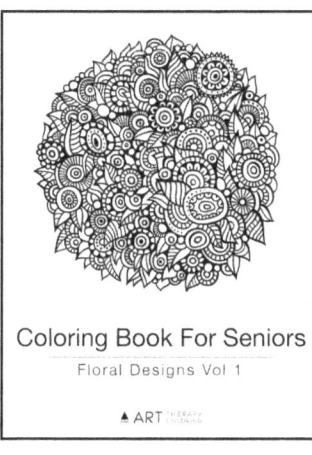

Coloring Book For Seniors
Floral Designs Vol 1

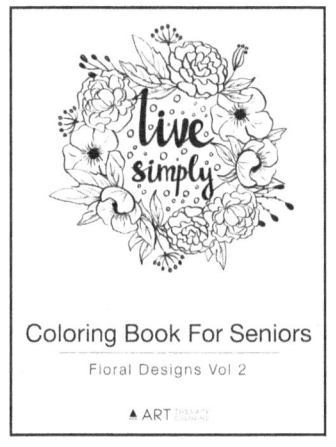

Coloring Book For Seniors
Floral Designs Vol 2

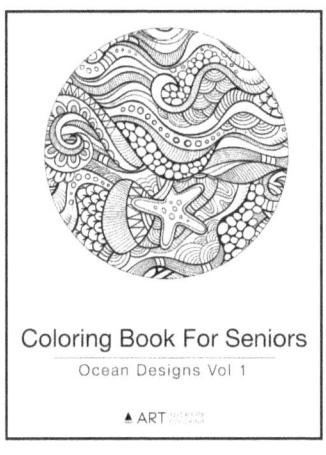

Coloring Book For Seniors
Ocean Designs Vol 1

# Coloring Books For Teens

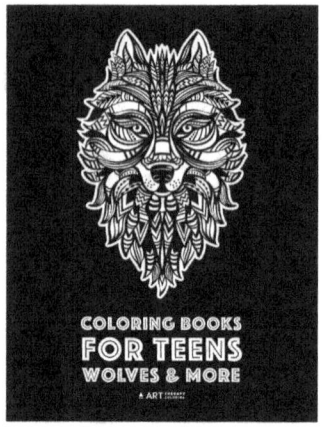

**COLORING BOOKS FOR TEENS WOLVES & MORE**

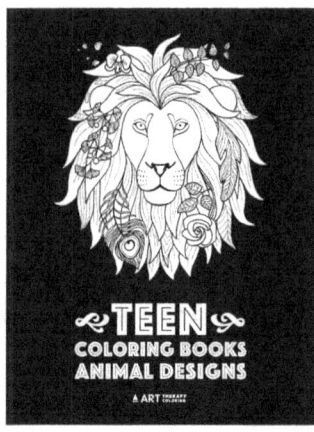

**TEEN COLORING BOOKS ANIMAL DESIGNS**

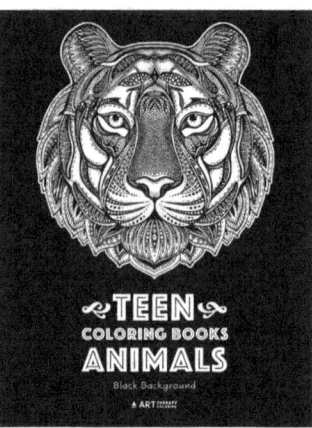

**TEEN COLORING BOOKS ANIMALS**
Black Background

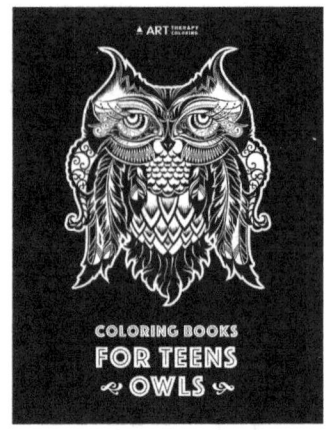

**COLORING BOOKS FOR TEENS OWLS**

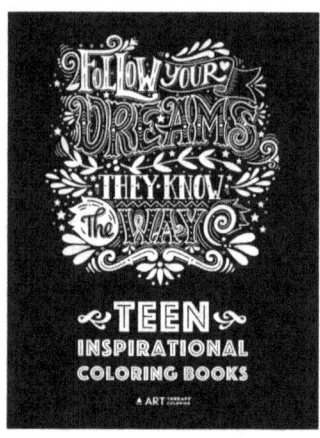

**TEEN INSPIRATIONAL COLORING BOOKS**

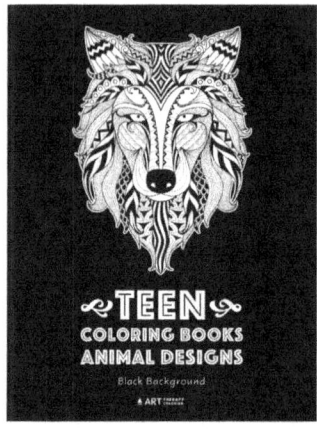

**TEEN COLORING BOOKS ANIMAL DESIGNS**
Black Background

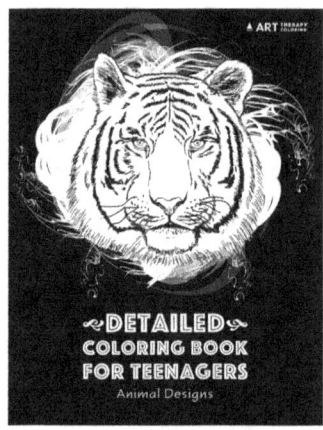

**DETAILED COLORING BOOK FOR TEENAGERS**
Animal Designs

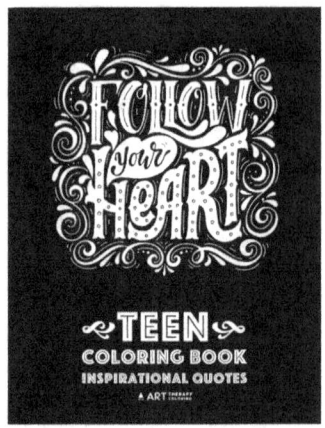

**TEEN COLORING BOOK INSPIRATIONAL QUOTES**

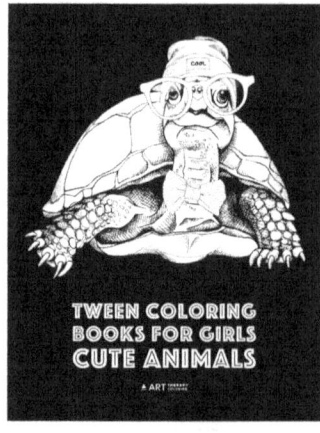

**TWEEN COLORING BOOKS FOR GIRLS CUTE ANIMALS**

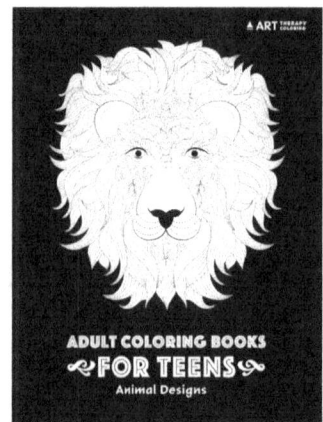

**ADULT COLORING BOOKS FOR TEENS**
Animal Designs

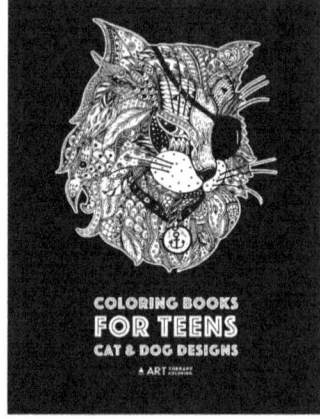

**COLORING BOOKS FOR TEENS CAT & DOG DESIGNS**

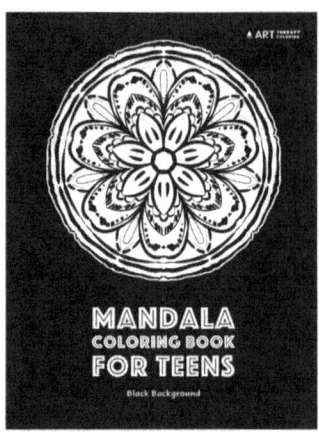

**MANDALA COLORING BOOK FOR TEENS**
Black Background

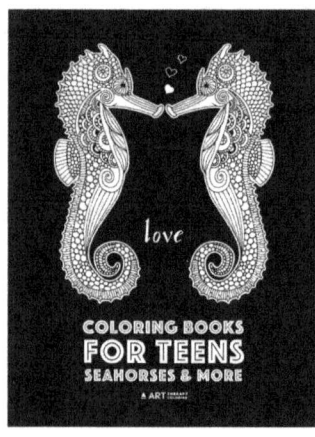

**COLORING BOOKS FOR TEENS SEAHORSES & MORE**

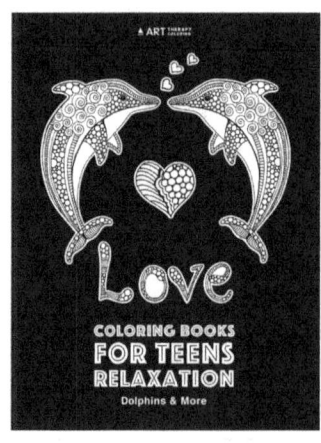

**COLORING BOOKS FOR TEENS RELAXATION**
Dolphins & More

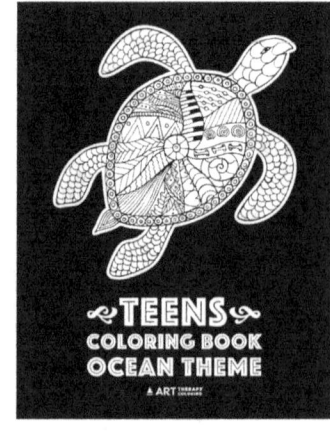

**TEENS COLORING BOOK OCEAN THEME**

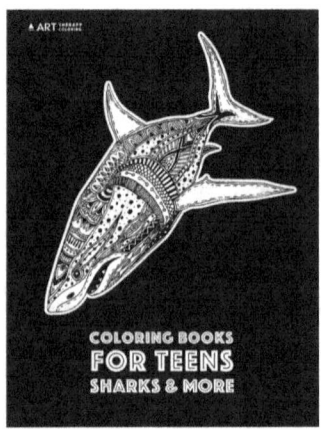

**COLORING BOOKS FOR TEENS SHARKS & MORE**

# Coloring Books For Teens

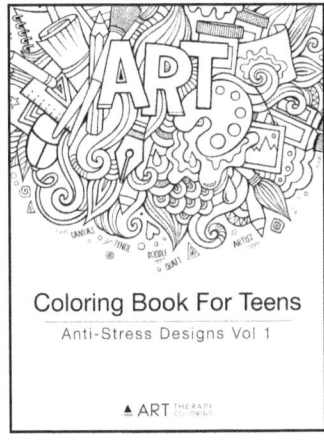

### Coloring Book For Teens
Anti-Stress Designs Vol 1

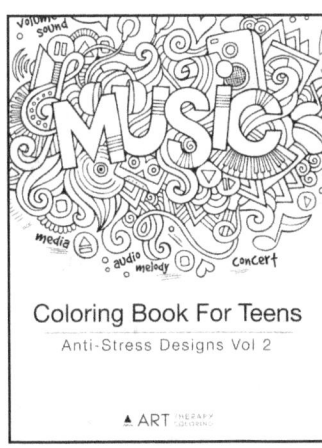

### Coloring Book For Teens
Anti-Stress Designs Vol 2

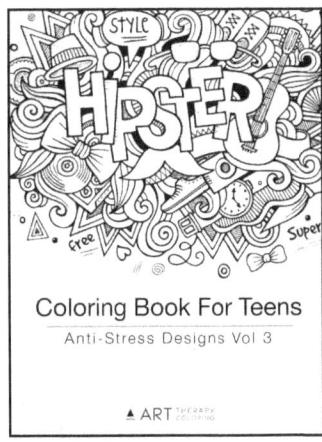

### Coloring Book For Teens
Anti-Stress Designs Vol 3

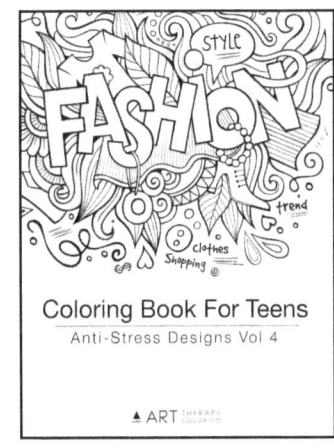

### Coloring Book For Teens
Anti-Stress Designs Vol 4

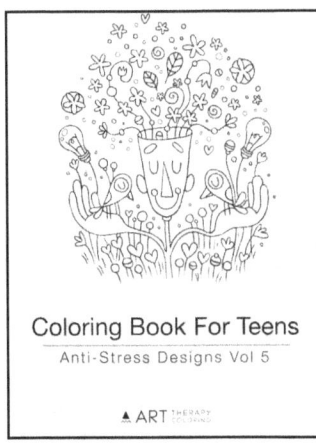

### Coloring Book For Teens
Anti-Stress Designs Vol 5

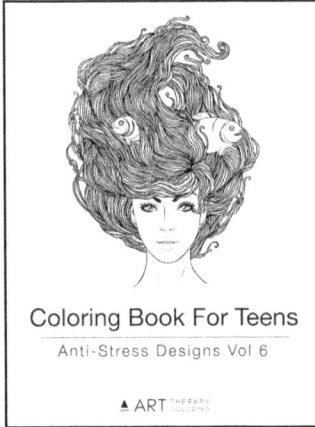

### Coloring Book For Teens
Anti-Stress Designs Vol 6

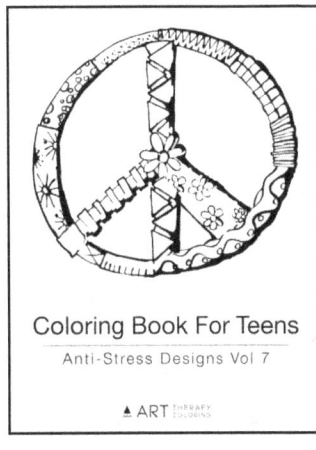

### Coloring Book For Teens
Anti-Stress Designs Vol 7

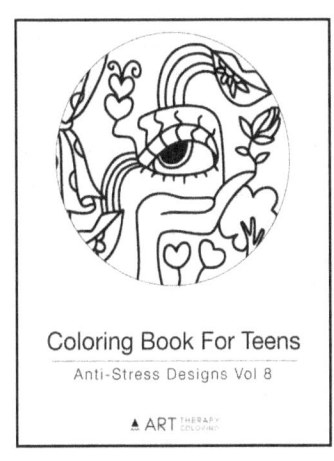

### Coloring Book For Teens
Anti-Stress Designs Vol 8

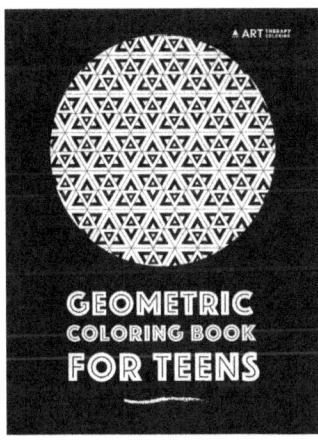

### GEOMETRIC COLORING BOOK FOR TEENS

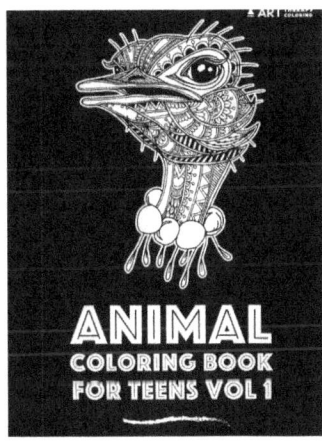

### ANIMAL COLORING BOOK FOR TEENS VOL 1

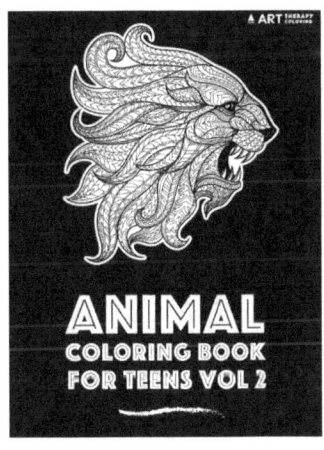

### ANIMAL COLORING BOOK FOR TEENS VOL 2

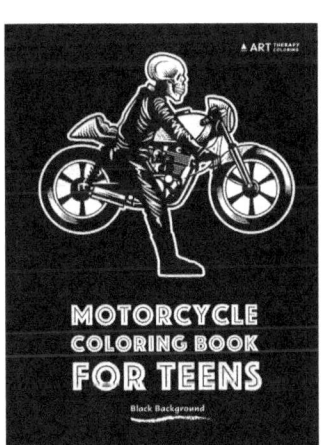

### MOTORCYCLE COLORING BOOK FOR TEENS
Black Background

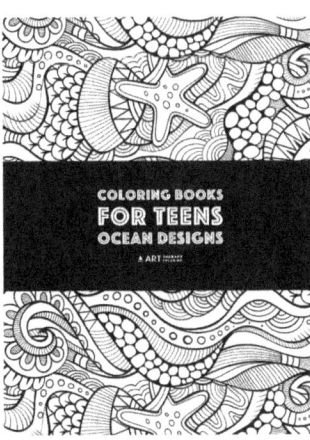

### COLORING BOOKS FOR TEENS OCEAN DESIGNS

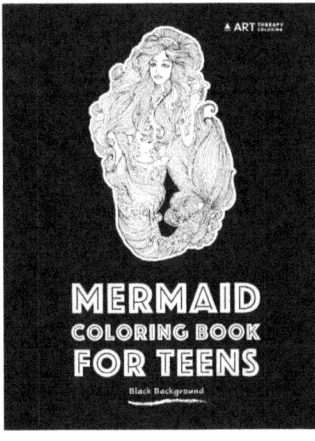

### MERMAID COLORING BOOK FOR TEENS

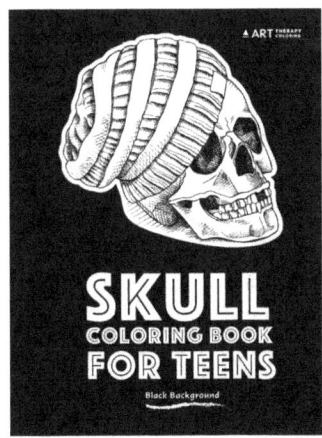

### SKULL COLORING BOOK FOR TEENS
Black Background

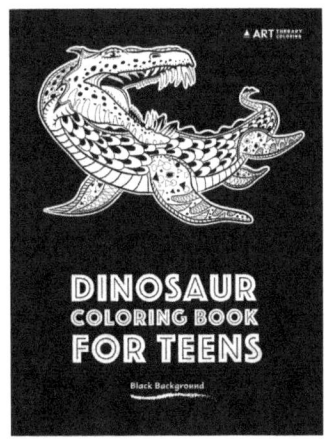

### DINOSAUR COLORING BOOK FOR TEENS
Black Background

# Coloring Books For Girls

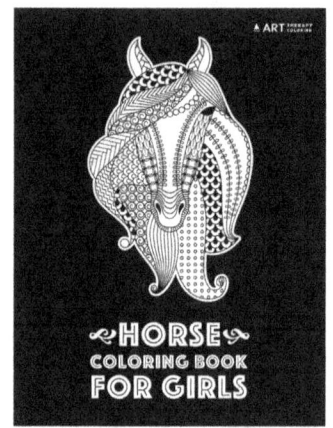

HORSE
COLORING BOOK
FOR GIRLS

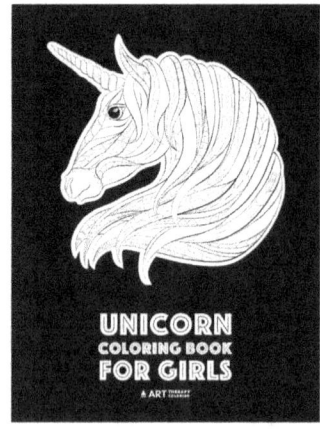

UNICORN
COLORING BOOK
FOR GIRLS

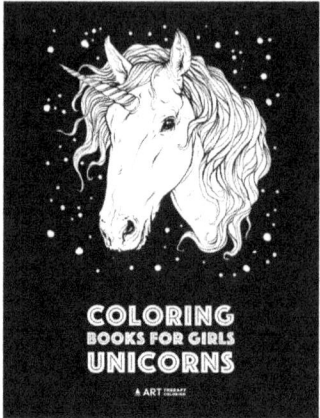

COLORING
BOOKS FOR GIRLS
UNICORNS

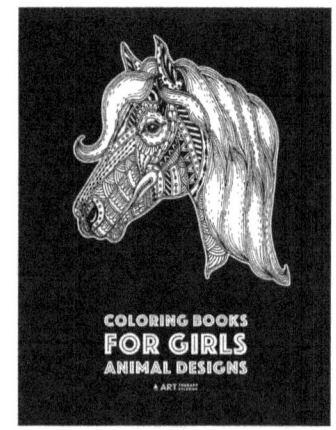

COLORING BOOKS
FOR GIRLS
ANIMAL DESIGNS

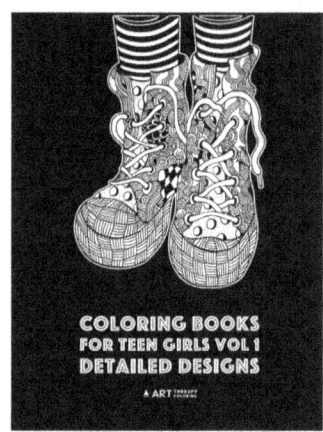

COLORING BOOKS
FOR TEEN GIRLS VOL 1
DETAILED DESIGNS

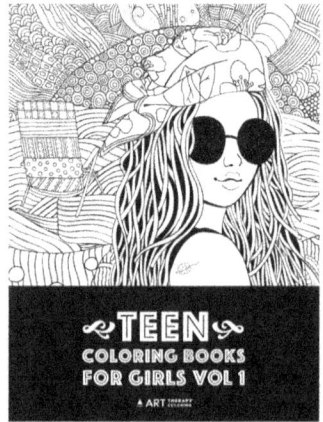

TEEN
COLORING BOOKS
FOR GIRLS VOL 1

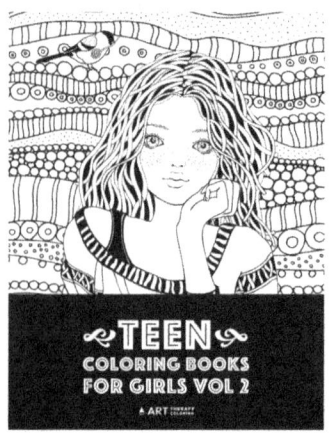

TEEN
COLORING BOOKS
FOR GIRLS VOL 2

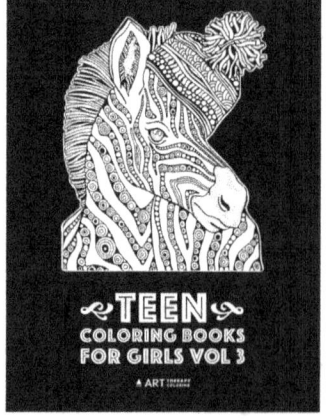

TEEN
COLORING BOOKS
FOR GIRLS VOL 3

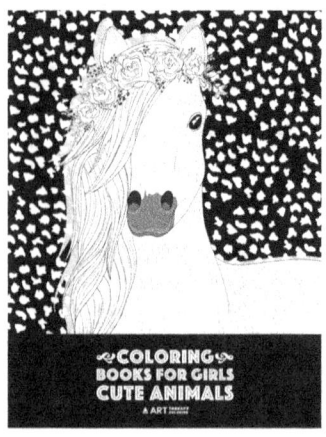

COLORING
BOOKS FOR GIRLS
CUTE ANIMALS

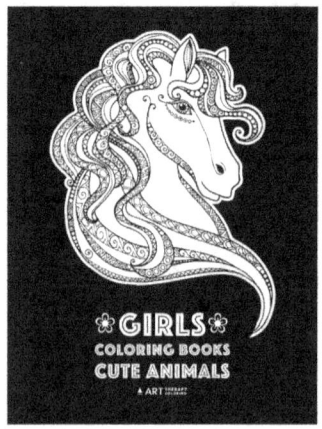

GIRLS
COLORING BOOKS
CUTE ANIMALS

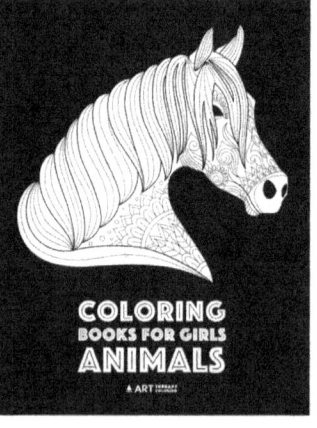

COLORING
BOOKS FOR GIRLS
ANIMALS

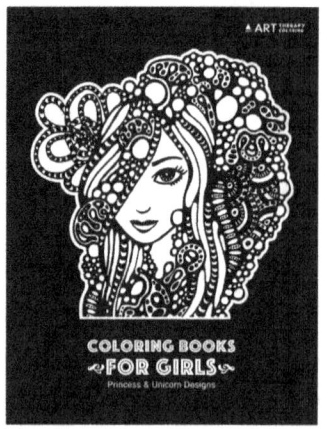

COLORING BOOKS
FOR GIRLS
Princess & Unicorn Designs

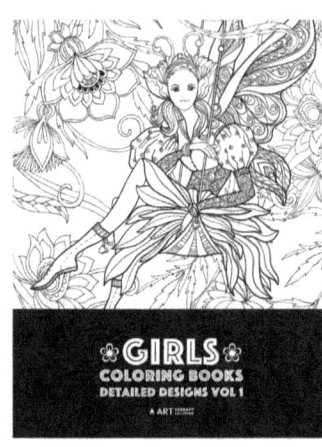

GIRLS
COLORING BOOKS
DETAILED DESIGNS VOL 1

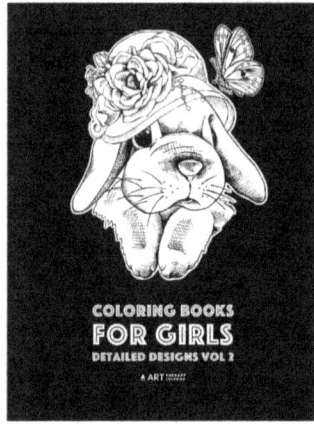

COLORING BOOKS
FOR GIRLS
DETAILED DESIGNS VOL 2

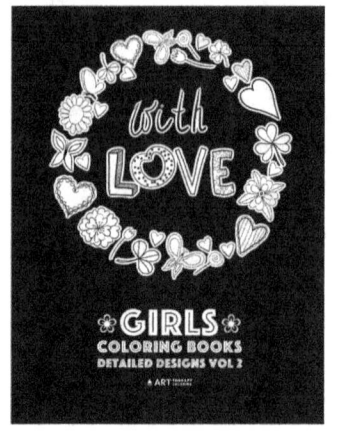

GIRLS
COLORING BOOKS
DETAILED DESIGNS VOL 2

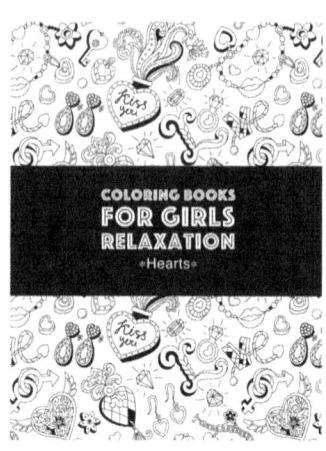

COLORING BOOKS
FOR GIRLS
RELAXATION
Hearts

# Art Therapy Coloring Books

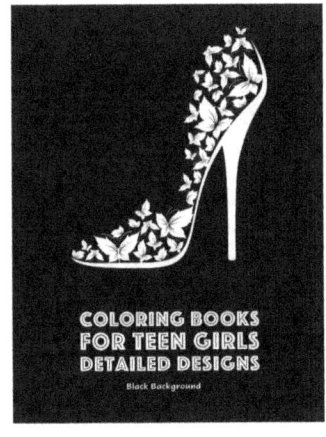

COLORING BOOKS
FOR TEEN GIRLS
DETAILED DESIGNS
Black Background

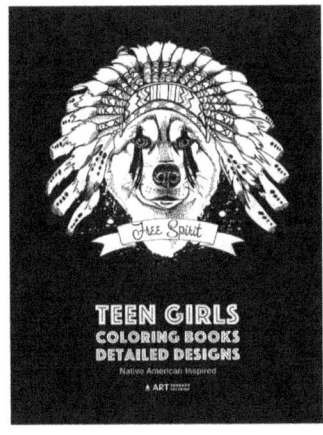

TEEN GIRLS
COLORING BOOKS
DETAILED DESIGNS
Native American Inspired

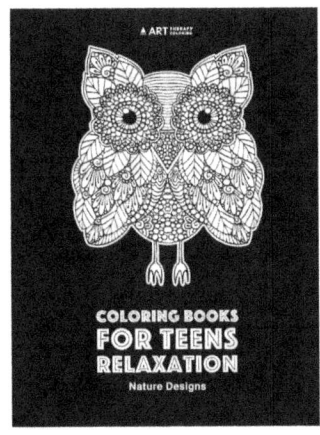

COLORING BOOKS
FOR TEENS
RELAXATION
Nature Designs

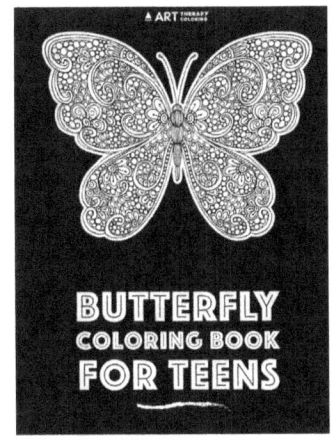

BUTTERFLY
COLORING BOOK
FOR TEENS

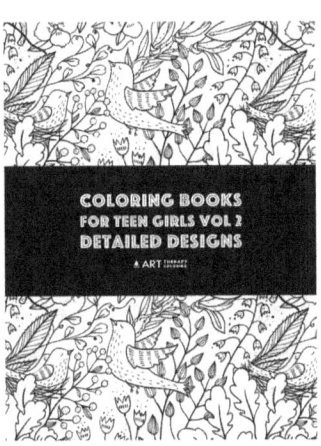

COLORING BOOKS
FOR TEEN GIRLS VOL 2
DETAILED DESIGNS

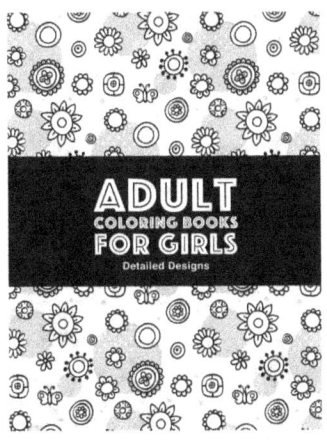

ADULT
COLORING BOOKS
FOR GIRLS
Detailed Designs

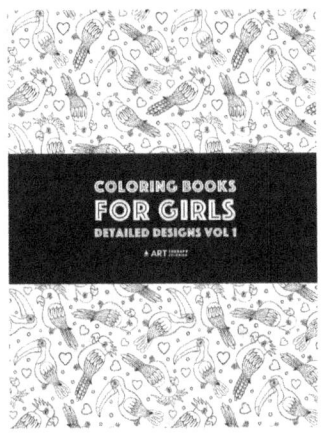

COLORING BOOKS
FOR GIRLS
DETAILED DESIGNS VOL 1

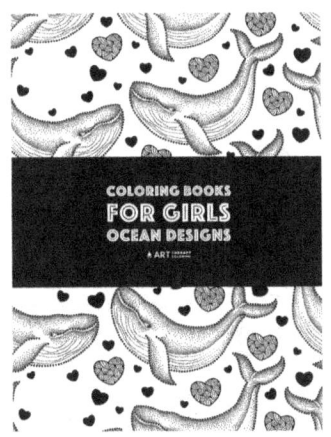

COLORING BOOKS
FOR GIRLS
OCEAN DESIGNS

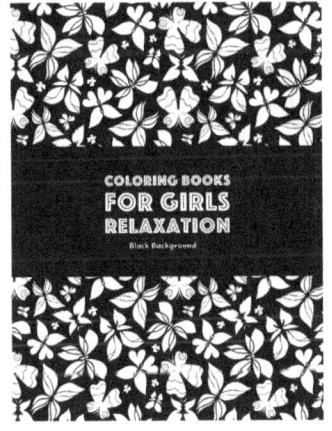

COLORING BOOKS
FOR GIRLS
RELAXATION
Black Background

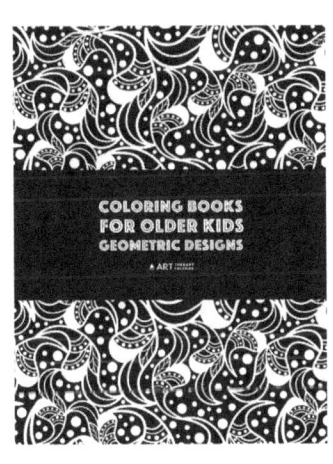

COLORING BOOKS
FOR OLDER KIDS
GEOMETRIC DESIGNS

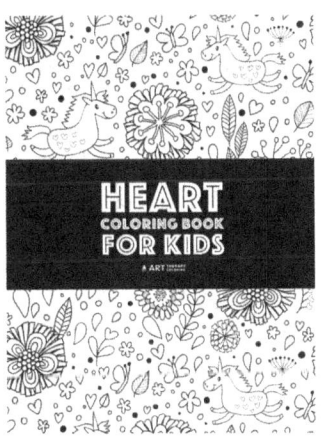

HEART
COLORING BOOK
FOR KIDS

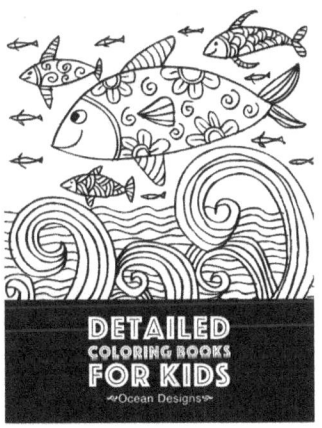

DETAILED
COLORING BOOKS
FOR KIDS
Ocean Designs

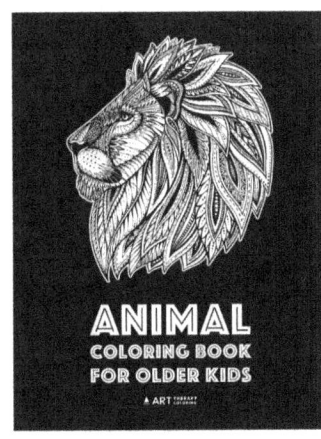

ANIMAL
COLORING BOOK
FOR OLDER KIDS

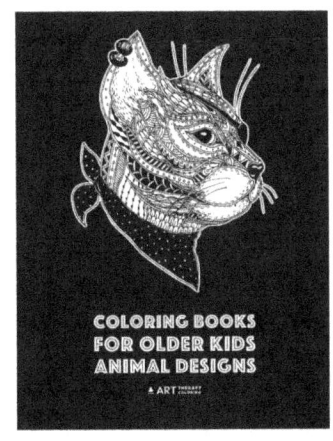

COLORING BOOKS
FOR OLDER KIDS
ANIMAL DESIGNS

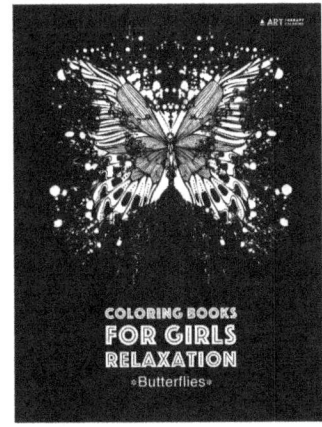

COLORING BOOKS
FOR GIRLS
RELAXATION
Butterflies

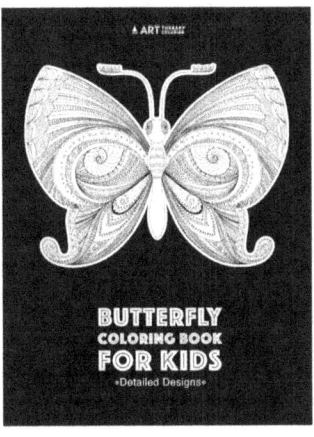

BUTTERFLY
COLORING BOOK
FOR KIDS
Detailed Designs

# Coloring Books For Boys

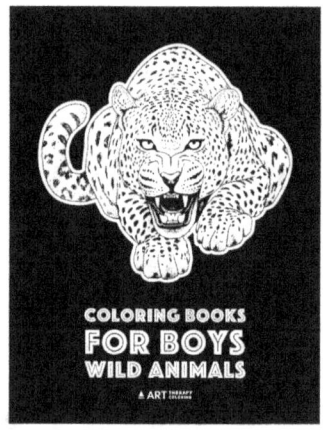

COLORING BOOKS
FOR BOYS
WILD ANIMALS

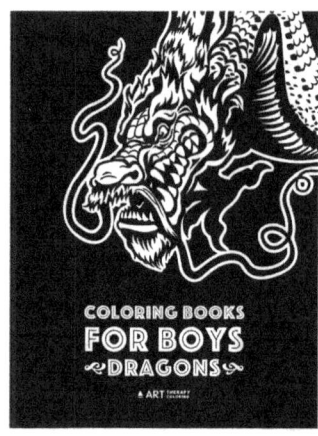

COLORING BOOKS
FOR BOYS
DRAGONS

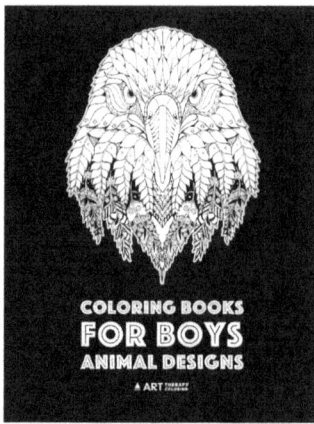

COLORING BOOKS
FOR BOYS
ANIMAL DESIGNS

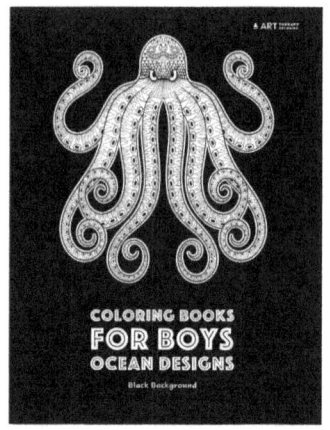

COLORING BOOKS
FOR BOYS
OCEAN DESIGNS
Black Background

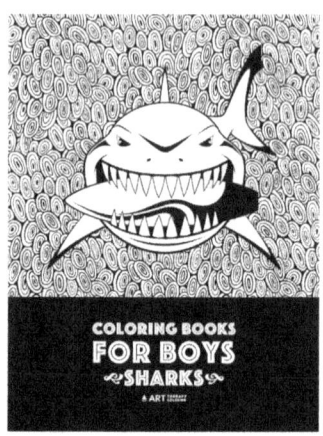

COLORING BOOKS
FOR BOYS
SHARKS

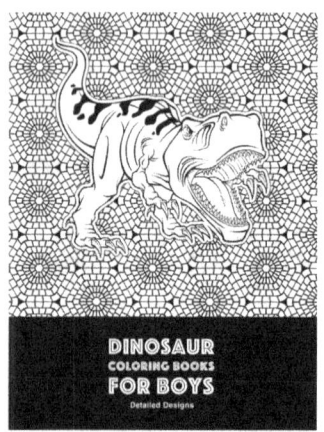

DINOSAUR
COLORING BOOKS
FOR BOYS
Detailed Designs

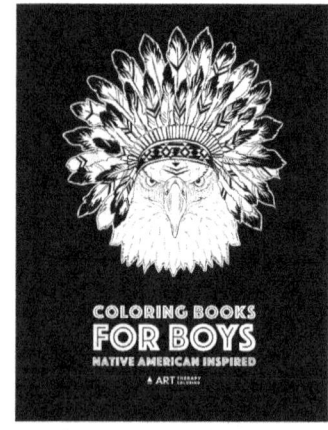

COLORING BOOKS
FOR BOYS
NATIVE AMERICAN INSPIRED

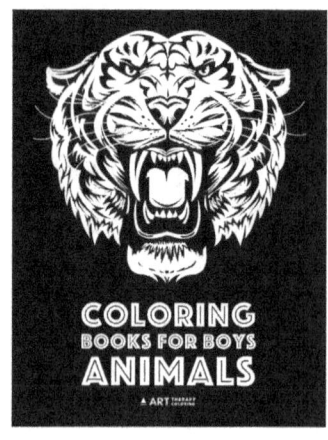

COLORING
BOOKS FOR BOYS
ANIMALS

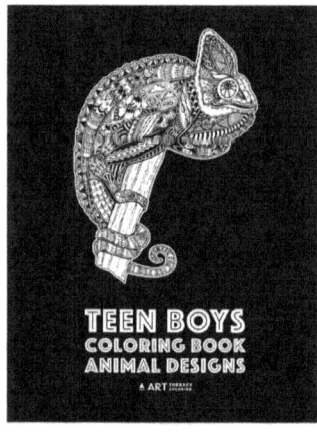

TEEN BOYS
COLORING BOOK
ANIMAL DESIGNS

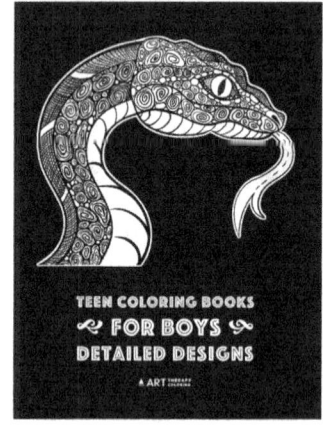

TEEN COLORING BOOKS
FOR BOYS
DETAILED DESIGNS

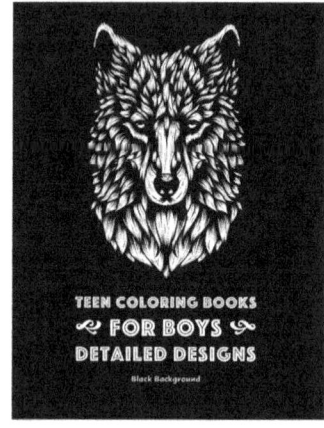

TEEN COLORING BOOKS
FOR BOYS
DETAILED DESIGNS
Black Background

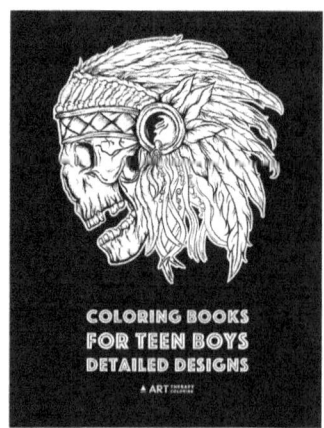

COLORING BOOKS
FOR TEEN BOYS
DETAILED DESIGNS

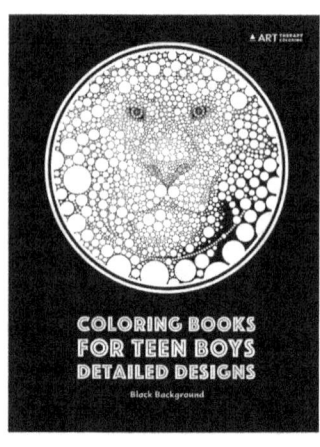

COLORING BOOKS
FOR TEEN BOYS
DETAILED DESIGNS
Black Background

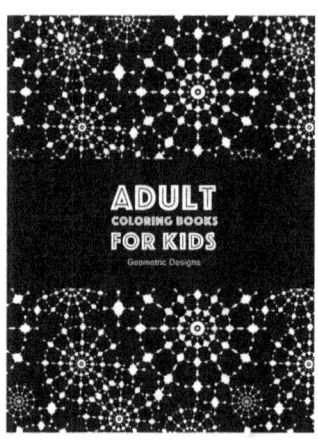

ADULT
COLORING BOOKS
FOR KIDS
Geometric Designs

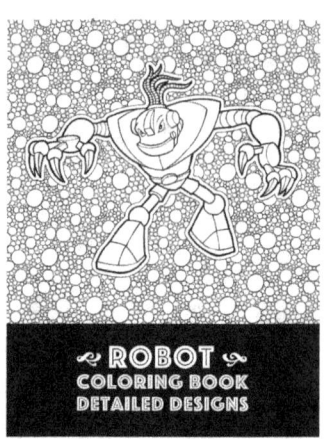

ROBOT
COLORING BOOK
DETAILED DESIGNS

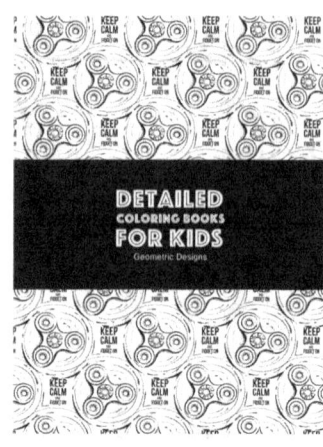

DETAILED
COLORING BOOKS
FOR KIDS
Geometric Designs

# Coloring Books For Kids

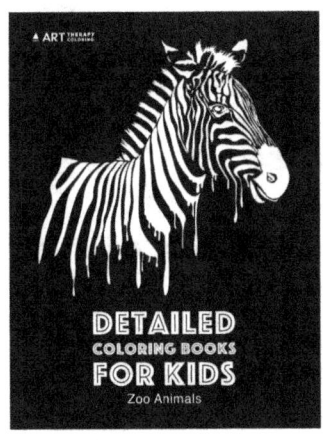

**DETAILED**
COLORING BOOKS
**FOR KIDS**
Zoo Animals

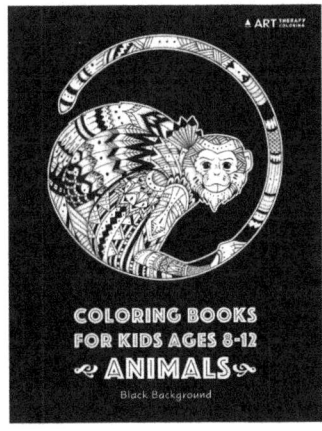

**COLORING BOOKS
FOR KIDS AGES 8-12
ANIMALS**
Black Background

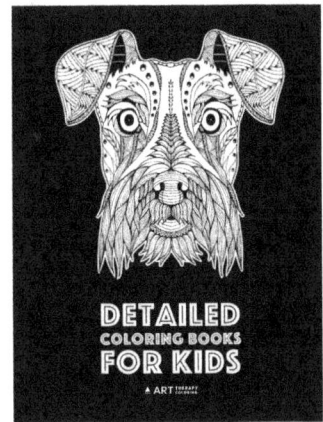

**DETAILED**
COLORING BOOKS
**FOR KIDS**

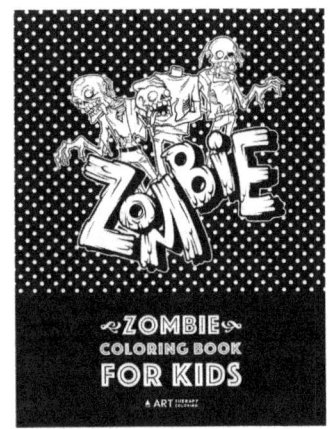

**ZOMBIE**
COLORING BOOK
**FOR KIDS**

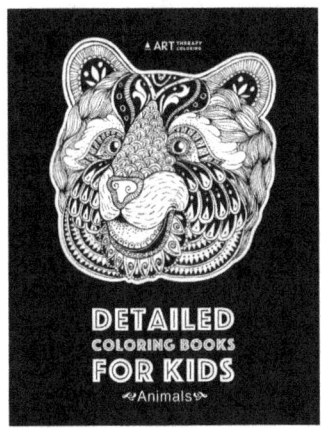

**DETAILED**
COLORING BOOKS
**FOR KIDS**
Animals

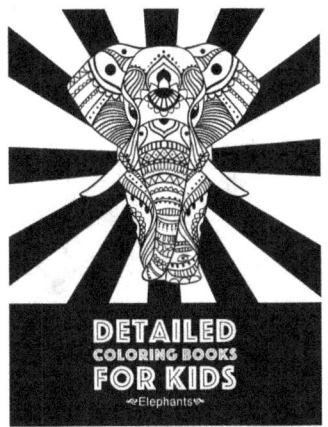

**DETAILED**
COLORING BOOKS
**FOR KIDS**
Elephants

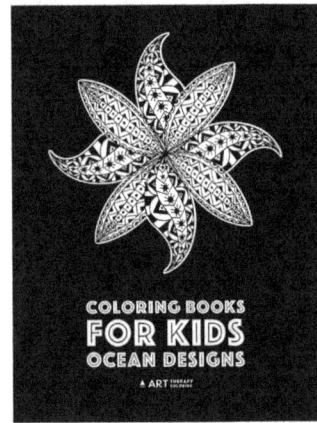

**COLORING BOOKS
FOR KIDS
OCEAN DESIGNS**

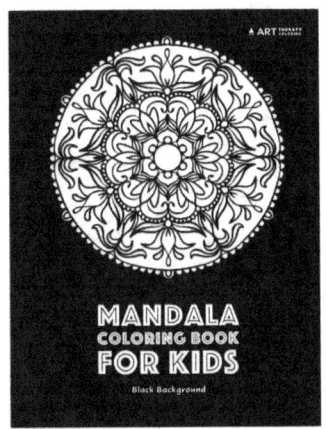

**MANDALA**
COLORING BOOK
**FOR KIDS**
Black Background

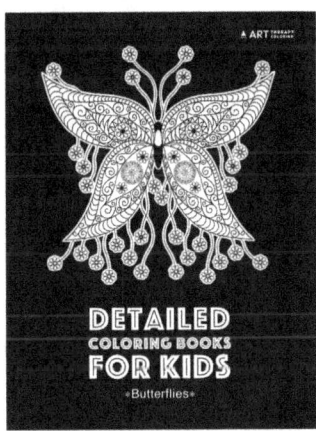

**DETAILED**
COLORING BOOKS
**FOR KIDS**
Butterflies

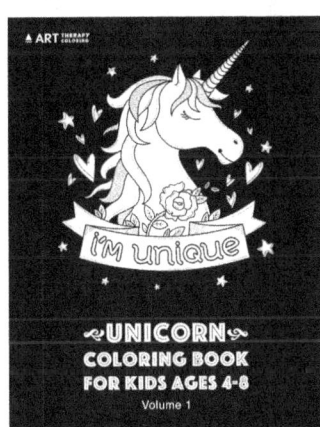

**UNICORN**
COLORING BOOK
**FOR KIDS AGES 4-8**
Volume 1

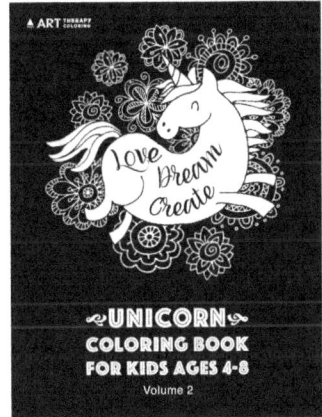

**UNICORN
COLORING BOOK
FOR KIDS AGES 4-8**
Volume 2

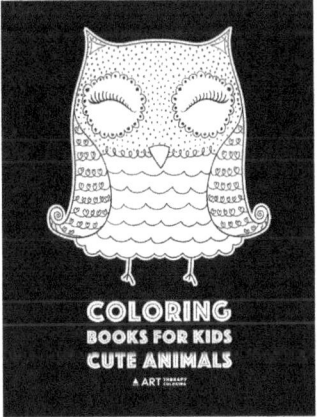

**COLORING**
BOOKS FOR KIDS
**CUTE ANIMALS**

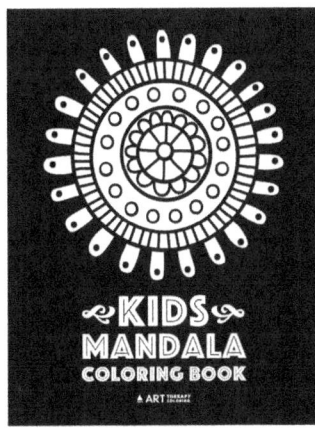

**KIDS
MANDALA
COLORING BOOK**

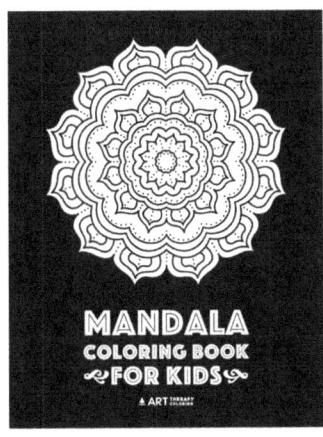

**MANDALA
COLORING BOOK
FOR KIDS**

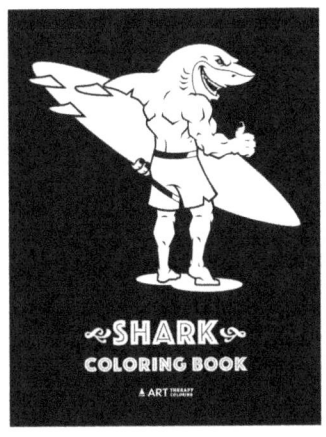

**SHARK**
COLORING BOOK

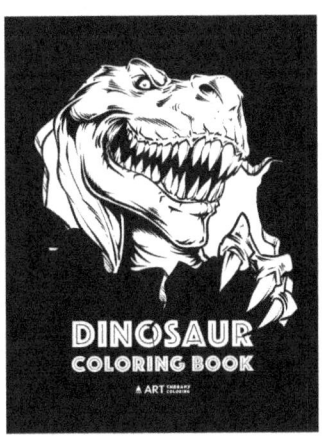

**DINOSAUR**
COLORING BOOK

# Coloring Books For Special Occasions

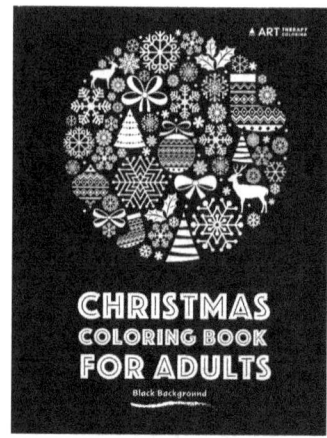
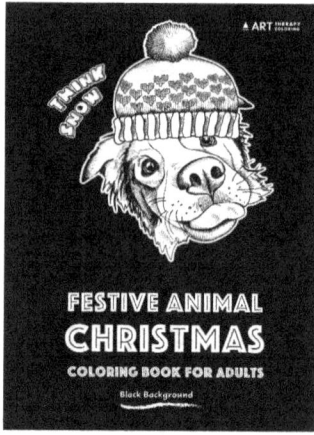
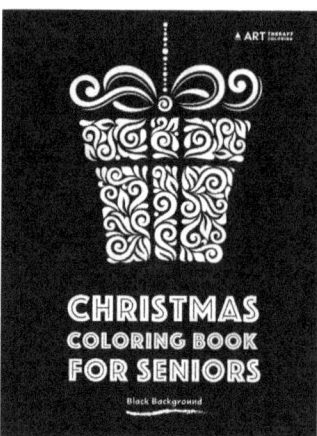
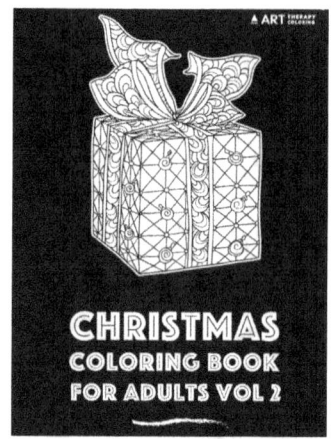

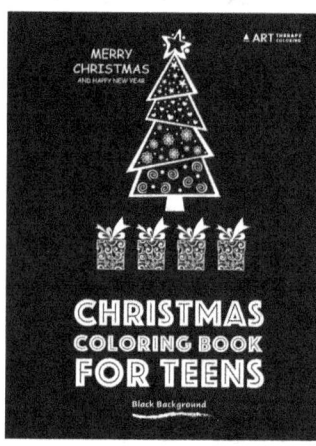
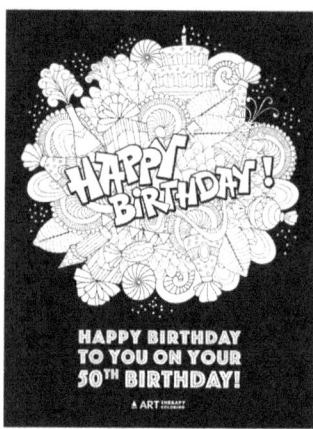
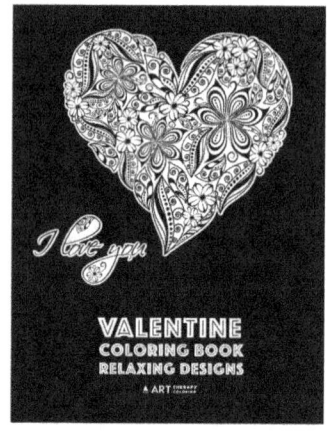
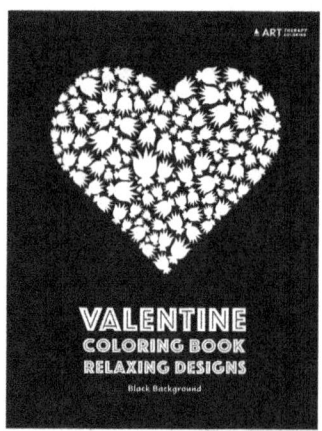

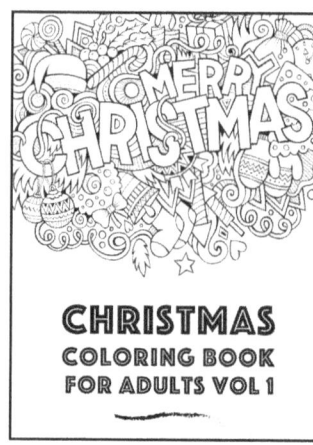
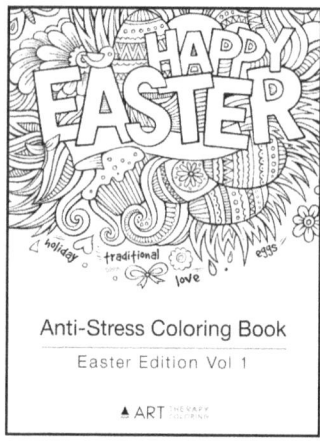
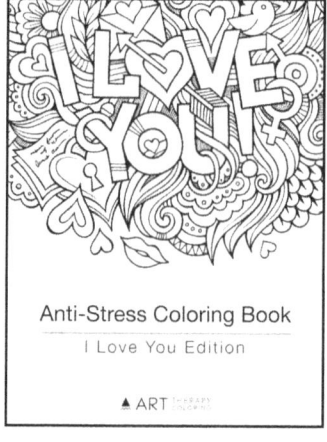
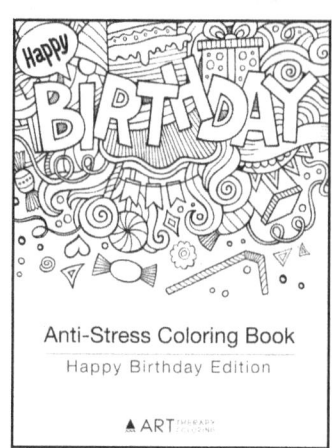

Owl Coloring Book For Adults

Published by:
Art Therapy Coloring
El Dorado Hills, California
www.arttherapycoloring.com

Shutterstock Images

ISBN: 978-1-64126-021-3

www.ingramcontent.com/pod-product-compliance
Lightning Source LLC
Chambersburg PA
CBHW081344180526
45171CB00006B/597